Landfall Walks I

BOB AC

A VIEW FROM CARN GALVER

An engraving by R. T. Pentreath,
published by Besley of Exeter during the 1850s.

Features
BOTALLACK, LEVANT, GEEVOR, DING DONG
and the other great western mines

Mining Trails in the Far South West

First published 1993 by
LANDFALL PUBLICATIONS
Landfall, Penpol, Devoran, Truro, Cornwall TR3 6NW
Telephone Truro (0872) 862581

Copyright © R.S.Acton, 1993

A CIP catalogue record for this book is available from the British Library.

ISBN 1 873443 09 9

IMPORTANT NOTE

I have done my best to ensure that all the recommended routes are on public rights of way, with a few unavoidable exceptions mentioned in the text, and that they are all unobstructed. If you come across unexpected difficulties (new fences, changed field-boundaries, rotted footbridges, waist-deep mud ....) please be patient, take the nearest practicable alternative route, and if possible let me know about the problem so that I can refer to it in any future edition of this book. Please help farmers and other landowners by leaving all gates as you found them, and by keeping dogs on a lead when there are livestock nearby.

USING THE BOOK

The boxed note at the start of each walk description is intended to be read before you set out; sometimes it would be useful to make preparations a day or two in advance in order to get the most out of the walk. A star (*) indicates that there is a boxed note on this point - usually but not always on the same page. The directions attempt to be very exact and explicit, but the maps are only rough sketches, so I'd strongly recommend taking with you the relevant Ordnance Survey maps. Landranger 203 (Land's End) covers all the routes. Best of all for walkers is the Pathfinder series; the sheet named "St Ives and Penzance (North)" includes all the routes except part of Walk 1, which is on the "Land's End and Newlyn" sheet.

FRONT COVER: "A View from Carn Galver" (1993),
pastel painting by Derek Jenkins
BACK COVER: Cape Cornwall from Kenidjack Castle (Walk 3),
photograph by Bob Acton

Typesetting, maps, drawings and colour photographs by Bob Acton

Printed by the Troutbeck Press
and bound by R. Booth Ltd., Antron Hill, Mabe, Penryn, Cornwall

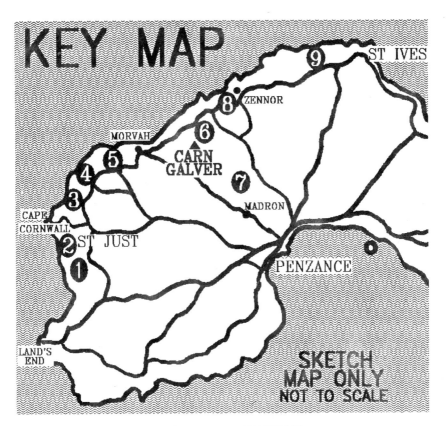

CONTENTS

INTRODUCTION

I would be amazed if anyone could visit the far west of Cornwall and remain wholly impervious to its special magic. Ever since I started this series of books I have looked forward to walking and writing about it. The only deterrent has been the thought that others have beaten me to it, notably Ian Cooke. The ancient sites of Penwith hold a great fascination, and it is not surprising that Mr Cooke should focus mainly on those in his walking guides. My own interest, however, has centred more on the industrial heritage, and the appearance towards the end of 1992 of a minutely detailed and very exciting study of the St Just mining region finally convinced me that there is a need for a book, based on that area, along the lines of *A View from Carn Marth* and *A View from Carn Brea*. The survival of so much evidence of early mining between Land's End and St Ives, together with the availability of published material and the expert knowledge of several people who generously offered their help - all this has encouraged me to probe more deeply than usual into the history of these fascinating and often spectacular sites. I realise that there is a risk of overloading a book like this with detail. The walks are all very fine in their own right, and I have tried to pay due attention to "points of interest" of all kinds. Readers who are resistant to the bites of the Cornish Mining Bug will probably skip whole paragraphs or even pages of what follows, but I hope to have succeeded in conveying some of my own enthusiasm.

"Carn Galva is the finest hill in the Land's End district", declared Murray's Handbook (1859). Although not the highest, it is the one which offers the best view of the area covered by this book, even if that view doesn't quite stretch to the furthest edges. To the east are the great mines of the St Ives district, to the west the even greater ones of St Just; prominent to the south is the Greenburrow engine house at Ding Dong, and close at hand to the north are the picturesque buildings of Carn Galver Mine. The stupendous cliff scenery of this stretch of coast; the valleys leading down to it - each with its own unique character and special beauty; the little grey towns and villages dominated by medieval churches and 19th-century chapels; the ancient granite farm buildings - many of them virtually hamlets in their own right - surrounded by fields whose patterns date back to the Iron and even the Bronze Age; the windswept moorland and rugged outcrops dotted with prehistoric monuments: all can be enjoyed on these nine walks.

ACKNOWLEDGEMENTS

This time - as will be very obvious even from a cursory glance at Walks 1-5 - my largest debt is owed to a book, the Cornwall Archaeological Unit's *St Just - An Archaeological Survey of the Mining District*. The small library of other publications which have contributed in large or small measure to my own are listed in the Bibliography. As always, I have received invaluable help from many people, notably Tony Bennett, Justin Brooke, Kenneth Brown, Joff Bullen, Bill Newby and Graham Thorne. Thanks, too, to Roger Penhallurick for making it possible, at an extremely busy time, for me to select from the Royal Institution of Cornwall's collection of historic photographs. All the black-and-white photographs in this book are taken from that collection.

SOME MINING TERMS

This book is written with the interested general reader in mind, rather than those who have made a special study of mining in Cornwall. Although some explanations of technical terms are included in the main text, I think a brief glossary may prove helpful. Please bear in mind, however, that these are very simplified explanations: several of these words have formed the basis of lengthy articles and even whole books.

ADIT   A drainage channel with its mouth or **PORTAL** in a valley or on a hillside or cliff face. In deep mines the water had to be raised by pumping to the level of the adit; this is why statistics often state the depth of a mine "below adit". Adits also often doubled as shafts by following the metal **LODE** (vein), and in some cases provided access for the miners.

BAL   An area of tin-working. Mines named Bal tend to be older than those called **WHEAL**, though this is certainly not a hard-and-fast rule. Oliver Padel (CPE) suggests that a Bal was generally a group of workings, especially on the surface, whereas a Wheal was a specific tin-work.

BEAM ENGINE   Thomas Newcomen of Dartmouth (1663-1729) was the first to develop a steam engine which could be used for pumping water up from the mines. The cylinder was placed vertically, and the piston was chained to one end of a massive wooden or cast iron beam or **BOB**, pivoted on a strong wall, known as the **BOB WALL**. The other end overhung the mine shaft and was attached by long rods to the pump at the bottom. In deep shafts the pitwork, as it was called, would have been too heavy for the beam to lift without the aid of at least one **BALANCE BOB**.   Balance bobs were

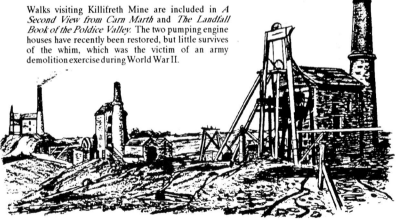

Walks visiting Killifreth Mine are included in *A Second View from Carn Marth* and *The Landfall Book of the Poldice Valley*. The two pumping engine houses have recently been restored, but little survives of the whim, which was the victim of an army demolition exercise during World War II.

Killifreth Mine, near Chacewater, some time between 1893 and 1897. The left- and right-hand engine houses, on Hawke's and Old Sump shafts respectively, were for pumping, and the rocking beams of the engines can be seen projecting from the bob walls. In the middle is the whim engine house, set at right-angles to the other two, so that its bob wall is hidden in this picture. The rotating drum, which is visible, would be used for hoisting and lowering in both the shafts.

small beams with one end attached to the pump rod and the other heavily weighted: when the rod descended the balance bob's weight prevented it from falling too quickly, and when it rose the weight helped it up. In the 1770s James Watt and Matthew Boulton began manufacturing an improved engine, and James Pickard modified beam engines to produce rotative motion, used mainly for the driving the whim and stamps. (See the entries on those.) Early in the 19th century, great improvements were brought by the use of high-pressure steam; the research and inventions of Richard Trevithick (1771-1833) made an important contribution here, but many other engineers also played a significant part. The size of each engine was expressed in terms of the diameter of its cylinder: 45", 90", etc.

BUDDLE A device for concentrating ore by means of gravity. Early buddles were rectangular, but in the 19th century most were circular; water containing the ore which had been reduced to a fine powder in the stamps was fed to the centre of a **CONVEX BUDDLE** or the sides of a **CONCAVE** one, and rotating brushes were used to ensure that the heaviest, metal-bearing particles settled closest to the inlet point. A more sophisticated form of buddle called a **ROUND FRAME** came into use in Cornwall in the 1870s. In this the bowl rather than the brushes rotated.

BURROW or **DUMP** A heap of mine waste (**DEADS** or **ATTLE**) - often very useful now as evidence of the mine's production. The burrows of many old mines have been "worked over" for valuable minerals which can be recovered by improved techniques.

CALCINER (pronounced "cal-*sign*-er") A furnace in which ore was roasted in order to drive off impurities such as arsenic and sulphur. If the arsenic was wanted, the fumes were passed though a long, zigzag flue known as a **LAMBRETH** (labyrinth), from which the deposits were collected.

COFFIN, COFFEN or **GOFFEN** One of many terms used for mining on the surface. A coffin or **GUNNIS** is a narrow, slot-like excavation; where a broader, quarry-like pit was dug the term used was **OPENWORK** or **BEAM**. The word **STOPE** normally means an excavated area underground, but is also sometimes used of surface workings.

COUNT HOUSE The mine's office.

DRESSING FLOOR The area where the ore was prepared for smelting.

DRY A building where mine workers changed their clothes. Photos exist of the big pipes connected to engine boilers which heated the dry at Levant.

FATHOM Six feet.

FLAT-RODS Wooden or iron rods which were used to transfer power from a steam engine or waterwheel to a remote location.

LEAT An artificial watercourse. Where a leat was carried in a raised trough it was known as a **LAUNDER**.

REVETMENT A wall built to support an earth bank.

SETT "The ground granted to a company of adventurers" (C. C. James) (**ADVENTURERS** were shareholders in a mining enterprise.) The word "sett" was also used for the granite blocks used to carry rails.

STAMPS Cornish Stamps machines were used to crush the small lumps of ore into material like sand in texture. Heavy timber or iron lifters with iron "heads" at the bottom were raised by cams on a rotating axle, and fell on the ore, fed into a box beneath. Small stamps were usually powered by waterwheels, as in the picture (taken from the Perran Foundry catalogue by courtesy of the Trevithick Society), and larger ones by steam engines.

STREAMING The normal method of winning tin before deep mining became possible. **ALLUVIAL TIN** washed down into valleys and buried under silt was exposed, originally by shovel and barrow; the tin-bearing gravel was then sorted and washed, and the waste material used to back-fill the excavated area. Nowadays, earth-movers and lorries do the work.

WHIM A machine for raising water, ore or other heavy materials from the mine. The earliest whims were operated by human beings or horses, walking round and round a flat circular area called a **WHIM PLAT** turning a wooden drum or capstan around which was wound the cable attached to the **KIBBLE** or bucket. Some **HORSE WHIMS** continued in use till the present century, but the whims in deep mines were driven by steam engines, and these were known as **FIRE WHIMS**. An improvement on kibbles were the steel containers called **SKIPS**; these were sometimes equipped with wheels and drawn up and down a **SKIP ROAD**.

A SERIES OF LINKED ROUTES WHICH YOU CAN ADAPT TO YOUR OWN NEEDS

I have designed a single round walk of about 16 miles which includes a wide variety of coastal and inland scenery - rural and urban, farmland and high cliffs, sheltered valleys and bleak moorland. Nearly all of it is attractive, and much of it breathtakingly beautiful or dramatic or both. The route visits almost every important mining site in the St Just district, the main exceptions being those that are on the east side of the B3306.

To most people, 16 miles sounds very daunting, particularly when about half of it consists of one of the tougher sections of the South West Way (coast path). Even if you are a seasoned walker who could manage it in a single day with little difficulty, I would not recommend you to try, because you need plenty of time to linger in and explore the places of historical interest - and there are literally scores of those.

The complete route is planned as a series of five walks of roughly equal length (between four and five miles), in such a way that you could do each one individually or combine them in groups of two, three or four. Since Walks 4 and 5 are "figure-of-8" routes with parking space near the point where the two halves of the "8" meet, they could in fact each be treated as two separate walks, thus further increasing the flexibility of the "St Just Mines Trail".

The start-and-end point of the complete Trail, the main car park in St Just, is also the base for Walks 1, 2 and 3, so one of the possibilities would be to do Walk 1 in the morning, returning to St Just for lunch, and complete the day with Walk 2 or 3 or both.

BUSES Most of the later part of the Trail runs fairly close to the main St Ives - St Just road (B3306). Except on Sundays, several buses per day operate along the section of that road between St Just and Portherras Cross, which is the junction with the Penzance road at Pendeen. If you are planning to set out from St Just on a longish walk it may be worthwhile to check the current timetables beforehand, just in case you run out of strength or time or both! Two or three times a day except Saturdays buses venture as far along the road as Morvah, going to or from St Ives, but only during the season.

REFRESHMENTS Except in St Just itself, you are very unlikely to find refreshments on sale anywhere along the Trail, although I presume that when the mining museum at Geevor re-opens, so too will its café. There are pubs, cafés and / or shops at Pendeen, Trewellard and Botallack village, most of which are quite easily accessible from the walk route.

Full directions for walking the St Just Mines Trail are included under the headings of Walks 1 - 5. **Bold type is used to help you pick out the links between the routes.**

8

THE ST JUST MINES TRAIL

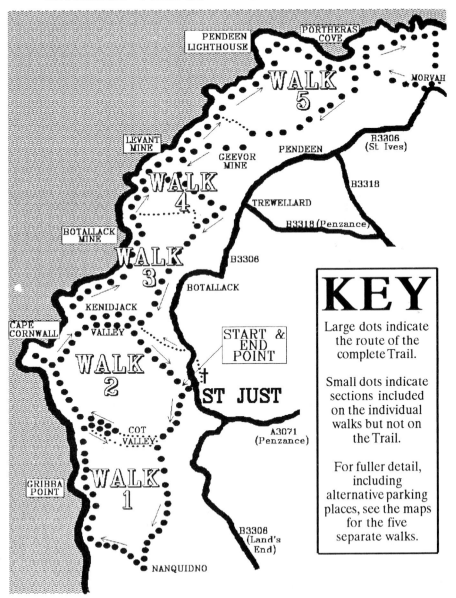

PENDEEN LIGHTHOUSE

PORTHERAS COVE

MORVAH

WALK 5

LEVANT MINE

GEEVOR MINE

PENDEEN

B3306 (St Ives)

B3318

TREWELLARD

B3318 (Penzance)

WALK 4

BOTALLACK MINE

WALK 3

B3306

BOTALLACK

KENIDJACK

CAPE CORNWALL

VALLEY

START & END POINT

WALK 2

ST JUST

COT VALLEY

A3071 (Penzance)

GRIBBA POINT

WALK 1

B3306 (Land's End)

NANQUIDNO

KEY

Large dots indicate the route of the complete Trail.

Small dots indicate sections included on the individual walks but not on the Trail.

For fuller detail, including alternative parking places, see the maps for the five separate walks.

WALK 1
THE ST JUST MINES TRAIL
SECTION 1:
ST JUST AND THE NANQUIDNO
AND COT VALLEYS

Nearly five miles

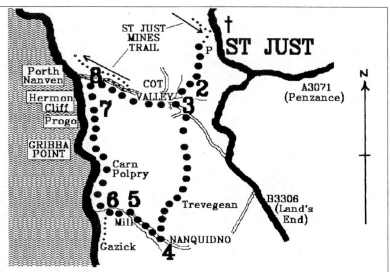

This is a walk amidst delightful scenery, including a fine stretch of cliffs and two very contrasting valleys, one of which (Nanquidno) is probably the prettiest of all the many valleys that run down to the coast in St Just parish. Somehow it manages to be almost "cosy", surrounded though it is by the Atlantic rollers on one side and the bare hills of the Land's End on the other. (Its alternative name, Nanjulian, could be translated as "valley nook", which seems apt.) There are fewer surviving mine buildings on this section of the "Trail" than the others, but the evidence of early mining activity is equally interesting if you know where to look for it. There are some rather steep climbs on the coastal part of this walk, and the field paths are likely to be muddy in places but in general the stiles are well maintained. Shops, pubs and toilets are all available in St Just, but not elsewhere on this route. Of the five pubs clustered in and around Market Square, the Wellington and the Star have been particularly recommended to me for their food. A useful companion on this walk would be Des Hannigan's "Wildlife Walkabouts: Land's End Peninsula, Cornwall", which includes a detailed account of the flora and fauna to be seen in the Cot Valley and on the high ground to the south.

ST JUST

'The village of Redborne is large, yet unattractive. .... The houses are scattered about over a large area; and in one place, where they are sufficiently numerous to form two or three streets, the collection has been dignified by the name of "town", though the reason is no clearer than why a triangular piece of ground in the centre should be called the "square".' (EBT) The novelist's unflattering description of St Just was more than matched by the Edwardian guidebook quoted by Gerald Priestland in WHR: "a dreary town that has seen better days, smug, commonplace ... without a trace of beauty or interest ..." The same writer could find "no redeeming features" in Hayle; enough said! John Betjeman got St Just right (just right), I think: "It is too workaday a place to be likely to be turned into a self-conscious tourist resort" - and that, of course, is part of its charm. Its growth from a small, predominantly agricultural community of under 3,000 in 1800 to an industrial town of 9,000 in 1870, and its decline to some 4,000 in the 1960s, have of course been directly related to the fortunes of its mines - including a china-clay works - and associated enterprises such as Holman's St Just Foundry at Tregeseal. (The population figures refer to the parish of St Just, and are taken from StJinP and StJP.) Having its own Mayor (and a Mayor, what's more, who's the only one in Britain with a chain of office made of tin), it can indeed be dignified by the name of "town". Churches dominate it - at least three big, impressive nonconformist chapels in addition to the parish church - and pubs to suit all tastes cluster around them. The churchyard, with its two ancient crosses and its gravestones that speak of the harsh realities of life - and death - in a mining parish, is overlooked by some of the most attractive granite cottages in the county. The church itself and the Plen an Gwary are the chief items of "beauty or interest" in the town, and there are separate notes on these in Walks 2 and 3. Although the Market Square / Bank Square area feels like the town centre, Chapel Road rivals it. The biggest Methodist Church is there - which was almost certainly attended by far larger congregations than the parish church at least in the 19th century, if still today: John Wesley in 1750 had judged his St Just following to be the biggest in the county, and over a century later "Edward Bosanketh" portrayed the "flock" of the Anglican vicar as being tiny (EBT). The primary and secondary schools are close by; so are the Town Hall and the Drill Hall. The latter still bears a plaque showing the symbol of the St Just Battery, whose rifle range was on the cliffs near Kenidjack Head, as mentioned in Walk 3. The town's big annual event, the St Just Feast, starts on the Sunday nearest to 1st November and continues for the following week.

Directions start from the main car park in St Just (*), which is on Market Street: approaching from the main Penzance road, turn left when you reach the Market Square at the centre of the town, near the church. There are public toilets at the car park.

1 Turn left at the main exit from the car park (opposite the Fire Station and Library on Market Street), and left again at the T-junction. This road,

Bosorne Terrace, takes you past the Methodist Free Church, built in 1860, when the prosperity of the local mines was probably at its height. (As mentioned later, that was also the year in which the Wesleyan Church at St Just was enlarged.) Continue past the playing field, and where the main lane curves left go on ahead, following the footpath sign to the Cot (or Cott) Valley. Carrallack Farm has the sturdy granite buildings typical of this area, and a well which looks as if it's still in regular use. The house opposite the well has a truly magnificent crop of ivy: I wonder what state the roof is in beneath that lot! Soon you get your first good view of the Cot Valley, with Cot Mill prominent.

2 Where the track turns right, cross the stile ahead (there is a Public Footpath sign) and take the path that runs straight down to Cot Mill. (Apparently there were in fact two mills, Lower Cot Mill and Bosaverne Mill.) The hill on the skyline on your left now is Carn Brea (not to be confused with the one near Redruth), "the last hill in England", at the top of which was a large chamber tomb; that has gone now, however, along with the tiny chapel of St Michael which was built on top of the cairn in the 13th century. There is a second stile to cross and a small wooden gate to go through, and after the flight of steps just past Lower Cot Mill you soon come to a minor road.

3 Turn left on that. Ignore the right turning, but take the unsigned footpath on the right which comes a few yards after a signed one on the left. It starts with some steps up, and continues between hedges. On the left quite close to the stile you come to next is a dump of mine waste, which along with a single shaft are remains of a small mine called Wheal Diamond or possibly Wheal Damsel. It appears to have been active in the 1870s. The building downslope which looks rather like a small engine house is a little reverberatory calciner probably built early this century when some of the dumps were re-worked; beneath the vegetation and rubbish surrounding it are concrete dressing floors. The calciner is of special interest to industrial archaeologists because it is built to a design more typical of the 18th century. A photograph and description of it by Bryan Earl can be found in the 1983 *Journal of the Trevithick Society.* Mr Earl states that "the calciner could be put back to work with only small repairs." (The ruins of a similar old-fashioned calciner also probably dating from about 1900 can be seen in the Porthmeor Valley: see Walk 6, point 4.) Continue ahead beside the hedge on your right for a few yards, then go diagonally left across the field to the next stile, of the cattle-grid type. Now go on in the same direction, cutting off the left corner of the field, to stile No. 3. Stile 4 is straight ahead, in the far corner of the next field; stile 5 had a metal bar over it and a low fence on the far side. Ahead now on the skyline are Sennen church and Land's End. Still continue in the same line, cutting off the left corner and walking by the hedge on the left. Stile 6 is on the left of a gateway, and stile 7 straight ahead. Now head just to the right of the terraced cottages at Trevegean. The path runs past them along the left side of the field. Cross stile 8, which has a wooden bar, and go on down to stile 9, a very small one on the right of a metal farm gate at the field corner. One last stile by another such gate brings you to a lane that passes Wesley Cottages (did one of the Wesley brothers stay there?) and farm buildings and brings you to the little road running down the Nanquidno

Nanjulian Mill

Valley. (I have not found an explanation of this name, but it is rather similar to Nanquitho in Sancreed parish, which means "valley of trees".)

4 Turn right. Here, at least in winter, among these pretty buildings and the great clumps of bamboo one is surrounded by the sounds of water; but this "sub-tropical" atmosphere lasts only for a few yards, and soon the little valley opens out. Nanjulian Farm makes a pleasing picture, despite the rusty corrugated-iron roof and the dilapidation of some of the outbuildings. Not far beyond that is the farm's corn mill, now converted as a house; the old waterwheel was, we were told, restored at least twenty years ago. The millpond, now dried out, was up behind the mill, and the course of the leat that fed it is still obvious.

5 Turn left beside Nanjulian Mill, along a path that runs among huge boulders. If you ignore, for now, the path going left and instead continue down towards the sea, you will find yourself among the remains of a mine's dressing floors. The most obvious feature is the stone wheelpit. The wheel drove stamps. Nearby are traces of buddles and settling tanks, and the revetted banks below the wheelpit may indicate the site of the tin yard. This plant was probably used by Boscregan Mine, one of many small mines in this area of which few if any written records survive. There are two other points of interest to the industrial archaeologist here. Firstly, the stone bridge that carries the upper path spans an openwork excavation, where miners followed a lode that ran close to the surface. Secondly, the low heaps of mine waste on the other side of the stream contain water-washed stone, which according to CAU are "clear evidence for streamworking". (Colour photo. 1)

You might find a short diversion along the coast to the south worthwhile. You could use the signed coast path, which ascends a flight of rough steps, or walk with care along the narrow cliff-edge path. Just beyond the point where that path re-joins the main one there is the flooded entrance to an adit, also part of Boscregan Mine. The boulder-strewn "beach" below this, known as the Gazick, was used by a seine fishery during the 19th century. As CAU points out, it seems to be a totally unsuitable place to try to land a boat, but there may have been some sand-cover then. Adam Sharpe refers to the ruins of a slipway and several buildings associated with the fishing station, but we didn't find them. Cyril Noall states that "several large iron rings may be seen in the rocks at the north end of the beach to which boats were formerly moored." The seine was apparently defunct by 1880, when the wooden roof of the "Gassac Fish Cellars" was advertised for sale. (CSS)

6 To continue the round walk, cross the two footbridges at the mouth of the Nanjulian stream. Just beyond the wooden stile are signs of mining on and around the cliff-edge, probably relics of a mine called South Levant or Heul Speed. Next the coast path runs a little way inland up to Carn Polpry (the name means "claypit", but what claypit there is or was here I don't know). From the seaward side of this in clear conditions there's a magnificent view. Behind are Sennen church, Sennen Cove and Land's End. The Longships lighthouse should be visible; in clear conditions so too should be its companion on the Wolf Rock, and further right on the horizon the Isles of Scilly. (Wolf Rock is about 11 miles away, and the Scillies almost 30.) The islands less than a mile out, sometimes called the Sisters, are officially the Brisons (named from the French word "brisant", "breaker, shoal of rocks, reef"). Edith Nicholas mentions a local belief that the islands were once used as a prison, and that the name derives from that. She also says they were a favourite picnic spot for young people in Victorian times. (StJP) The wreck of the brig "New Commercial" on the Brisons in January 1851 is famous because of the outstanding bravery shown by the men who eventually managed to rescue the captain and his wife, stranded on the rocks of Little Brison. Along the coast to the right are Gribba Point and in the distance Cape Cornwall. Close at hand down to the left are a couple of fenced shafts, proably more relics of South Levant. The path descends quite steeply above Polpry Cove. Another small mine, Wheal Bull, is thought to have been situated here, and if you look back as you climb towards Carn Gribba you will see two openings just below the grassy cliff-edge on the far side of the Cove, with a heap of what looks like mine-waste at the foot of the cliff. There are in fact four such openings, according to CAU. At the top of Carn Gribba is a stone stile, and from there the path runs towards Carn Leskys ("burnt tor") and Hermon Cliff, with Progo Cove (from the Cornish *porth-googoo,* cove of the cave) below - easily recognisable by the natural arch at its northern end. Evidence of old mining ventures in the form of shallow pits and trenches is becoming more obvious now. In the 19th century this area was worked by mines called South Wheal Rose, Wheal Oak and Carnleskis.

HERMON CLIFF

The richness of this quite small area in terms of mining remains can be gauged by the fact that six A4 pages of maps and small print in CAU are devoted to it. Here the coastline runs roughly at right angles to the direction of the metalliferous lodes, so that they show up particularly clearly in the cliffs. The first attempts were made to follow these deposits inland a very long time ago: Wheal Hermon and the nearby Progo are, Justin Brooke tells me, the first Cornish mines ever to be named on a map (about 1560), and there is no reason to suppose that they were new enterprises then. At the other end of the time-scale, some work was done here as recently as World War I, when Wheal Hermon was still active. There is, however, hardly a trace of any sort of mine building nearby, and certainly no evidence for the use of steam engines: such power as was required for machinery (mainly for hauling ore up to the clifftop) was apparently all provided by horses and the water brought by the leats from the Cot Valley. Hence Adam Sharpe's claim that "there are few stretches of coast in Penwith where the walker is brought face to face with pre-industrial mining technology in quite so dramatic a fashion" as here.

7 Fork left, downhill, following the coast path acorn sign. A little further down, where the coast path turns left, you could use the narrower path straight ahead. Before rejoining the main path this takes you past the first of the remarkable gunnises for which Hermon Cliff (*) is celebrated among students of early metal mining. Back on the main path, you soon pass an awe-inspiring open shaft, then a deep adit on the right, from which a trickle of water runs, followed by three more gunnises, some of them visible down to the left as well as on the right. It is worth continuing down past more deep cuts to the boulder-strewn beach, known as Church Rock or Nanven Cove, where the entrance to one mine-working (colour photo. 3) has been surrounded by a massive stone wall. Sets of what appear to be bolt-holes in at least two rocks seaward of that (colour photo. 4) intrigued me: could they be evidence of wooden platforms or other structures that once projected from the cliff? A more likely explanation, perhaps, is provided by Edith Nicholas in StJP when she writes about the Midsummer Eve festivities that took place last century, when miners "would drill a train of holes in a rock, sometimes as many as twenty, and having charged them with black powder, would arrange trails of powder grains from hole to hole, so that as soon as the safety fuse fired the first hole, all succeeding holes would pop in succession." Examples of such "merriment holes" can, she adds, be seen on many of the local carns; maybe some of the seashore rocks provided useful practice. See also the comment on miners' drilling competitions in the note about the Plen an Gwary in St Just. To continue the walk, take the low path around the small headland. Notice the way the sea has sculpted the rocks below into soft-looking curves and hollows, like some huge eiderdown; and then on the other side of the point the complex patterns of crisscross lines in the rocks above tide level. The path soon brings you round to a footbridge over the stream in the Cot Valley (*). Beside it are the concrete foundations of a Pelton wheel which was used to drive dressing floors; notice how water was brought down from the leats (by pipe) to power this operation. A Pelton wheel is a type of dynamo that runs at high speed and requires a good head of water.

8 To continue the St Just Mines Trail, cross the bridge and walk up the valley road. After about a quarter of a mile, turn sharp left, following the coastal footpath sign. Now pick up the directions at point 3 in Walk 2.

To complete Walk 1, climb the steps beside the stamps foundations and turn left on the path above, then keep to the higher path. The concrete dressing floors on the other side of the valley, including a convex buddle, are relics of fairly recent mining. You will also see adit portals and shallow excavations beside the road, as well as heaps of mine waste, and several ruined buildings half-buried in vegetation nearer the stream, remains of earlier mining operations. On this side ran the long leats that served the many waterwheels in the valley and on and below the cliffs; in places the courses of these leats have been obscured by later mining, or they have been adapted as paths or

THE COT VALLEY

By comparison with the coast of Cornwall, the valleys which run down to it are little known to walkers; many of them, in fact, are almost impenetrable, or if they lead to a good beach are spoilt for walking by busy roads. They can be places of great beauty, however, with micro-climates which encourage plant and animal life in total contrast to the cliffs close by; and for those interested in mining history almost every one of them in areas such as the one dealt with in this book is fascinating. The Cot stream was undoubtedly a source of alluvial tin over many centuries (CAU mentions references in documents); it requires a practised eye to find evidence on the ground, but some small dumps of a shape known as "whaleback", containing water-rounded stones, have survived near the mouth of the stream, and what Adam Sharpe describes as "the massive scarps on the valley sides" show "how much of the valley bottom has been scoured away." The streamers would have used the flowing water to wash the tin-bearing gravel they recovered after any necessary stamping in machines driven by waterwheels, but all remains of these operations have been obliterated by the elements and later industry. The Cot Valley is exceptionally rich in remains of stamping mills and dressing floors; most of them date from the middle of the 19th century but some are clearly more recent than that: for details see pages 154-5 in CAU. That survey is particularly interesting in its study of the leats on the southern slopes, "which give an exceptionally dramatic impression of the long importance of water power in this mining district." Four main leats are identified, the lowest of which are entirely within the valley and may be associated in part with early tin streaming, but the highest two not only supplied the tinworks in the valley but also ran round the headland to serve waterwheels on and below the cliffs. The top leat begins well to the north of the Cot Valley, bringing in water from a smaller stream near Bosorne Farm. In a few places the water from the adits of mines on the south side, such as Letcha, the Reens and South Wheal Rose, was probably fed into the system. Maximum use seems to have been made of every drop of water, with many ponds holding reserves, and the tailrace from one waterwheel being led to another at a lower level wherever possible.

tracks. The one you're walking on leads up to a house (Cot Valley Lodge). The substantial ruined walls down by the stream once enclosed dressing floors; a big wheelpit has survived. Continue along the main path for a while, passing through part of the area once worked by Letcha and the Reens mines. Where the main path dips down to meet the valley road, take the uphill path, following the green arrow and YHA sign painted on a telegraph pole.

9 At the road turn left and follow the stream down among cottages, then up to join another path at a T-junction. Turn right there, and return to the car park by the same route as you began the walk.

Cottages beside the churchyard, St Just-in-Penwith

WALK 2
THE ST JUST MINES TRAIL
SECTION 2:
ST JUST, THE COT VALLEY,
CAPE CORNWALL AND THE
KENIDJACK VALLEY (SOUTH)

Nearly five miles

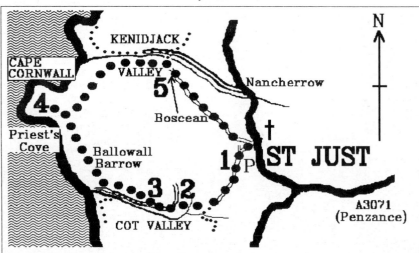

My impression that this walk and the two that follow are among the most magnificent that Cornwall has to offer is, no doubt, coloured by the fact that the weather at the time I researched them for this book (the last day of 1992 and the first two of 1993) was ideal. Surprisingly warm sunshine soon melted the thick frost, and the atmosphere was crystal-clear except on the third day. There was little wind, but big seas foamed around the rocks far below and boomed in the caves..... All this may be of little interest to you if it's now August, foggy and raining, but in almost any conditions these walks have much to offer, especially if you share my fascination with Cornish mining. Scenically this is perhaps the most satisfying and varied of all the walks I have linked to form the "St Just Mines Trail", since it starts and ends with contrasting valleys, between which come fine cliffs (affording exceptionally exciting long views) and one of the county's deservedly most famous places, Cape Cornwall. It also includes the most impressive prehistoric monument in the St Just district. There are few if any steep climbs on this walk, and you are not likely to encounter problems with mud or overgrown paths or stiles. As with Walk 1, shops, pubs and toilets are all available in St Just, but not elsewhere on the route.

Directions start from the main car park in St Just: details as for Walk 1.

1 Follow the directions in the first section of Walk 1, but this time ignore the stile ahead, overlooking Cot Mill: keep to the main track as it turns right, and continue ahead as it becomes a path and slopes down to meet a minor road.
2 Turn left on that. After a few yards it curves right and heads down the Cot Valley towards the sea. (See the boxed note about the Cot Valley in Walk 1.) Continue along the road for a quarter of a mile or so.
3 Take the signed coastal footpath - a widish track going up on the right which soon passes a surprisingly fertile-looking vegetable garden, islanded amidst the bracken. Higher up are waste heaps and many shafts, unusually close together. Looming ahead is the tall, rather insecure-looking chimney which was once part of the whim engine house of Bosorne and Ballowall Mine (*) (colour photos 5 & 6). The coast path runs well to the left of this stack; I suggest that instead you go a little further inland to join the minor road that runs beside it. This brings you, a short way beyond the stack, to one of the most impressive prehistoric monuments I know of, the magnificent Bronze Age chambered cairn known as the Ballowall Barrow (*) (colour photo 6). Continue to the end of the road, rejoining the coast path as it approaches Priest's Cove and Cape Cornwall. The few buildings that border the road as it runs down to Priest's Cove and the walled shaft nearer the sea belonged to the Little Bounds part of St Just United mine (*). The tiny,

A tin stamping mill just below what is now Cot Valley Lodge, photographed in 1905. A waterwheel, fed from one of the leats that ran along the south side of the Cot Valley, can be seen at the seaward end of the taller building, which housed the stamps. This mill probably processed ore from Letcha Mine and the Reens, up on the hill, which was presumably delivered via the steep chute. Three large buddles were sited between the mill and the stream, and their wooden superstructure is clearly visible in the picture.

BOSORNE AND BALLOWALL MINE

"The describing of an area of mining remains as complex, multi-phased and overgrown as Ballowall has proved a truly daunting task," writes Adam Sharpe (CAU) - and, believe me, he is not easily daunted! There are good reasons for supposing that the area along the north side of the Cot Valley and as far along the coast as Carn Gloose was mined in prehistoric times, and mining was still going on as recently as the 1940s. A bewilderingly large number of small mines were at work at different times, most of which were known by various names (seven variations on "Ballowall" are listed, for example), and they worked in several different combinations. During some periods in the latter part of the 19th century they were a part of St Just United or St Just Amalgamated - see the later note. Although so few recognisable mine buildings have survived, there is ample evidence among the furze and bracken and along the cliffs and valley-sides to show how intensively the area was worked: CAU mentions 17 adits and 106 shafts - but how many others have escaped attention so far? "The ground on this common," wrote R. M. Ballantyne in *Deep Down* (1868), " is so riddled with holes of all sizes and shapes, utterly unguarded by any kind of fence, that it requires care on the part of the pedestrian who traverses that place even in daylight." There may be more fences now, but the warning is still very relevant.

BALLOWALL BARROW

The name is said as "Bal-owl". Perhaps the word is linked with "bal", a mine, but I have not come across an explanation of it. John Norden (c. 1584) mentions "Ball-luholl" in St Just as one of the main mines of Penwith: see TTB. The barrow is sometimes referred to as Bollowall, Carn Gluze or Carn Gloose. An old photograph of the cairn, with structures of St Just United Mine including a horse whim in the background, is included in CNJ and MIC; surprisingly, both Cyril Noall and Jack Trounson thought the barrow was "coffins, or ancient surface workings"! In fact it is a huge and, so far as is known, unique chamber tomb of very early date - Neolithic and Bronze Age, probably about 2,500 - 1500 BC. The central chamber, which originally seems to have had a dome-like roof, contained several stone coffins (but not the sort Noall and Trounson meant!); it is surrounded by a massive wall, 8 feet high in places and 20 feet thick, apparently of later date, which has an entrance grave set into it. Ballowall Barrow, long buried twenty feet under mine dumps, was excavated in the 1870s, and that could well have been when the photograph I have just mentioned was taken. The excavators, described by Aileen Fox as a gang of miners, did a lot of reconstructing, and built a new wall around the central chamber so that it could be viewed more easily. The brief item on Carn Gluze in CAH says it "was discovered by the antiquarian Borlase in the 1870s" - but of course this was not the famous William Borlase of Pendeen and Ludgvan, who died more than a century earlier. The man in question was a descendant, W. Copeland Borlase. For a detailed description of this site, see ASDC. Borlase wrote a blow-by-blow account of the "dig" which was published in the Journal of the Royal Institution of Cornwall in 1878-81; Ian Cooke gives a lively version of it in JTS, along with some speculation about the ceremonial significance of the cairn.

ramshackle winch-house and fishermen's huts above the slip at Priest's Cove are worth a closer look. The huts are known locally as "crows" - the word rhymes with "cows" and means "hovels". Notice, too, the small bathing pool that has been created among the rocks, and the evidence of early mining in the west-facing cliffs above the beach. ("The coastal stopes on Saveall's Lode in Priest's Cove is one of the most dramatic and accessible of this type of feature anywhere in Cornwall," according to CAU. The gate at its entrance, fitted by the National Trust, does not prevent you from seeing how large these workings are.) The name of the cove is unlikely to refer to a clergyman, despite the closeness of a chapel in early times. Des Hannigan suggests it may derive from a Cornish word for meadow (NT11), but Charles Henderson saw it as a corruption of "Porth Just", "P'r East" (CHN). (Compare the old name of Gorran Haven, Port East, which refers to the tiny church there, dedicated to St Just.) This explanation is also supported by Oliver Padel (CPE). Continue up the impressive flight of steps. The way up to the mine stack perched with perfect aesthetic judgement on the summit of the Cape is obvious, and a National Trust sign offers you the choice of steep and gentle ascents. Unsurprisingly, the stack was part of Cape Cornwall Mine (*). When looking north-west from there you can clearly make out the remains of leats on the cliffs on the southern side of the next (Kenidjack) valley. Cape Cornwall's old name was Kilguth East ("East" again referring to St Just); the honour of being called a Cape is said to derive from the fact that it was once believed to be the most westerly point on the English mainland, marking the boundary between the English Channel and St George's Channel.

CAPE CORNWALL MINE

Though much restored in later years, the famous chimney on the summit has been there for nearly a century and a half. Originally it was linked by a long flue to a winding-engine house on the south side, but the draught it created was too fierce for the boiler, and a smaller stack just above the engine house was built to replace it. It had proved a useful navigational aid, however, and was kept. Jack Trounson in 1982 described it as "in a bad state of repair", but it was restored in 1986 by the National Trust. Mining probably took place on the Cape quite early, but Cape Cornwall Mine dates from 1836; it then worked, intermittently and sometimes under different names, till 1875. Its last active period was as part of St Just United (1879-89). Old photographs taken from Priest's Cove or the cliffs to the south reveal a scene scarcely less spectacular than the Crowns at Botallack, with the headgear of the pumping-engine house on the very edge of the cliff at the tip of the Cape. Apart from the stack, and the imposing count house beside the path leading up to it, little now remains of the mine's buildings. The long walls enclosing terraces below the count house look remarkably similar to some mine buildings elsewhere - the Vanner House at Wheal Basset, Carnkie, for example - but in fact they were built as part of a vinery. This is, though, where the mine's dressing floors were. Another relic that has survived is the base of a small circular gunpowder magazine like the two at Botallack; it is close to the path but hidden by vegetation. Kenneth Brown tells me that the cylinder bolts of the 40" pumping engine out on the headland are still visible in the path that leads round to the coastguards' lookout.

ST JUST UNITED MINE

This name was first applied to the many small - and in some cases probably very ancient - mines immediately south of Cape Cornwall in 1861; confusingly, the same name had earlier been applied to a group of very small mines in the Portheras area. Further confusion results from the fact that the southern St Just United worked as St Just Amalgamated for twelve or thirteen years. Several photographs have been published showing a mass of mine buildings and machinery overlooking Priest's Cove: good examples are photos No. 1 and 2 in MIC, - two of the most surprising old pictures of the St Just area, I think, because it requires a sharp eye now to detect any evidence of all that industry on the clifftop. The mine had a chequered history in the 19th century, with quite short bursts of large-scale activity. There were some failed attempts to re-work the mine or its dumps in our own century, but the last significant phase in its history was the 1880s, when its underground levels were combined with those of Cape Cornwall Mine, extending inland to St Just town and under the sea to the Brisons. The likelihood of making big profits with a venture like this can be gauged by the fact that the company had to fence off and make safe literally hundreds of old shafts and surface workings, and pump nearly forty million gallons of water out of the deeper shafts and levels that had been abandoned in 1875. Even the discovery of a huge "shoot" of tin ore, as much as 60 feet wide and 150 feet high, and so rich that it was nicknamed the "Cream Pot", failed to save the mine from the effects of falling prices, and it closed in 1889. Just before that, a novel called *Tin* was published, which focused mainly on a mine called Redborne Consols, in reality St Just United, and caused such consternation by its highly plausible portrayal of corruption in high places that every available copy was bought and burnt by the powerful Bolitho family. (See the Gulval walk in *A View from Trencrom.*) For anyone who values the opportunity to understand the St Just mining landscape in terms of the men and women who created it, *Tin* is essential reading - luckily, it is also very entertaining. See EBT in the Bibliography.

4 To continue the walk, you have to return along the road on the southern side of the Cape. In a field on your left is a small farm building on the site of St Helen's Chapel, sometimes called St Catherine's Oratory. The small cross on it looks old, but "was placed there in modern times" (NT11). Ahead is Porthledden House, built by Francis Oats (1848-1918), a Botallack miner who, having achieved impressive exam. results in Mineralogy, went out to the South African diamond mines, grew rich, returned home and bought Cape Cornwall in the early 1900s. (His photograph is in LCCM, on page 5.) Signs now proclaim Porthledden House to be a hotel, but it looked very deserted in the winter when we were last there. The rather forbidding buildings further right are those of Nanpean Farm; further right again is what looks like a large gunnis or small quarry. The coast path continues below the hotel's grounds, in which there appear to be old mine burrows or the remains of quarrying, and past a lonely house named Wheal Call, with its magnificent view across Porthledden Cove. ("Porthledden" probably means "wide cove". For Wheal Call, see the note on Boswedden Mine in Walk 3.) Soon the coast path curves inland at the seaward end of the Kenidjack or Nancherrow Valley,

Pay-day at St Just Amalgamated, photographed by J. Moody of Penzance in 1873. This mine was known at other periods as St Just United. Notice the boys among the work-force (though some of them may have been there to collect their fathers' or even their mothers' pay). Several of them are in the group perched on the roof to ensure that they featured prominently in the photograph. Notice too the studied nonchalance of most of the poses, which had to be held for a long time to avoid blurring on the very slow photographic plates of that period. Scarcely a trace remains on the clifftop above Priest's Cove now of any of the buildings in the foreground. The "bob" or beam projects from the engine house on the far right, linked to a large flywheel. In the distance is Cape Cornwall Mine. The long, curving flue linking the whim engine to the stack on the top is visible. On the right side of the whim engine house is its boiler house, now converted into a dwelling. Further right is the mine's count house, with roofed dressing floors below. The little round building further right again is the explosives magazine, much of which has survived. It is interesting to compare this photograph with the later one on page 68 in <u>CNSJ</u>: by that time a smaller chimney had been built just above the Cape Cornwall engine house, as mentioned in the boxed note, and a new engine house stood beside the headgear of Bailey's Engine Shaft at St Just United.

giving you a bird's-eye view of the massive wheelpits and other surface remains of Boswedden Mine, which are visited on the next walk. The building on the clifftop opposite is not an engine house: for details see Walk 3. As you walk further inland, notice the pattern of small square or triangular fields on the opposite slopes - probably a survival from very early times. (CAU mentions the "well-developed terraced field system" which "may be prehistoric in origin.") Ahead in the valley-bottom are the ruined buildings of the arsenic works, its tall stack wearing an odd little crooked cap. (See the note about Boscean Mine, and also the one on arsenic works in the next walk.) Where the coast path divides, carry straight on, continuing at the high level. Soon this brings you right above the arsenic works stack. On the other side of the valley are the buildings of Kenidjack Farm and hamlet, including the winding/pumping engine house of Wheal Drea (again visited on the next walk); much less complete but still a prominent landmark further inland is the stamps engine house of Wheal Grouse, which like Wheal Drea became part of Wheal Owles; and close at hand is the small stack of (Lower) Boscean Mine (*). (Hereabouts when we did this walk we chatted with a man - about 60 years of age, I'd guess - who told us that he was born less than three miles

BOSCEAN MINE

An important lode of copper and tin, very unusual in that much of it runs north/south instead of north-west/south-east, was mined under the sea by the Crowns section of Botallack, and it also lies beneath the Boscean district. This is one of the oldest mining setts in the area, mentioned in 1584 by John Norden, and during the 19th century it was worked on a large scale, employing at least seven beam engines. The chimney of one engine house and the ruins of the arsenic works are still important landmarks; beside the Kenidjack stream are remains of water-driven stamps and dressing floors; but surprisingly little else can now be seen on the surface. More than meets the eye has probably survived, however, buried beneath dense scrub and the dumped farm rubbish near Boscean hamlet. Two incidents of special interest took place in 1857 and about ten years later. On both occasions, miners at Boscean accidentally broke into other workings. Two men drowned that first time; the second accident killed no-one but resulted in heavy losses for Boscean, because Wheal Owles alleged "theft" of 15 fathoms of mineral ground, and Boscean was not only fined £600 but forced to hand over a section of its own workings, Lower Boscean, complete with all fixtures and fittings. The injustice of this became all-too-apparent over 25 years later, long after Boscean had closed, when one of the worst disasters in Cornish mining history afflicted Wheal Owles because of its own purser's failure to make accurate plans of the mine's workings. See the note on Wheal Owles in Walk 3. The arsenic works in the valley is of special interest because the remains include those of a Brunton calciner and "lambreth" flues much older than the famous ones at Botallack. Arsenic works always had tall stacks in order to create the necessary draught, but the extra-tall one here was built, I presume, in the hope of reducing the effects of noxious fumes in the valley; and the unusual cowl, which looks as if it may soon drop off, is supposed to have been needed because of the risk of downdraughts in this particular setting, or to direct the fumes away from crops on the nearby hillside.

away and had worked as a miner at Geevor till it closed. Now that he had some time to spare he was exploring the area and was bowled over by all the things he was seeing. Only yesterday he had visited the Cot Valley for the first time! On the other hand, he was quite familiar with Bavaria .....)

5 As you approach the stack, **to continue the St Just Mines Trail take the track on the left that winds down to the bridge, and follow the directions for Walk 3, starting at point 2.** To return direct to St Just, keep to the upper track, which curves right and passes among the houses of Boscean (Cornish, "dwelling in the dry place", pronounced "B'seen"), among which is a small pottery. Now the track becomes a minor road. Notice what, to judge from its name, is the former count house (offices) of Boscean Mine, on the right. (According to <u>CAU</u>, "The Old Count House was at SW 3633 3215" - i.e. this place - which implies that the present building is of later date.) Soon after you enter St Just you will pass the Cape Cornwall School (comprehensive), and nearby on your left is the large Wesleyan Methodist Church, built in 1833 and enlarged in 1860 to accommodate anything up to a thousand people. ("Emigrants say that the big chapel at St Just is the last piece of the Old Country they see as the liners from Southampton and Plymouth turn on their straight course for America, and the first they see on their return" - so wrote the Superintendent of the St Just Circuit on the occasion of the chapel's centenary.) Continue ahead at the crossroads, and you will come to Bank Square. On the right, beside the war memorial clock tower, is the Plen an Gwary (*). Take the path through that, and turn right at the street to return to the car park.

PLEN AN GWARY

This is a fascinating place with a very long and varied history. Ian Cooke argues that its origins may be prehistoric, since its shape and size are typical of many ancient ceremonial circles, and its Bank Square entrance faces the midsummer sunrise (<u>JTS</u>). Certainly it is at least medieval, and as an arena for the performance of plays - five manuscripts of Cornish "miracle plays" have survived - it was once just one of many in Cornwall. All but one of the others exist now only on paper and in place-names like Plain an Gwarry in Redruth and Playing Place on the Truro-Falmouth road; Piran Round near Perranporth is the only other one still intact and still occasionally used as a theatre. (See Walk 3 in *A View from St Agnes Beacon.*) The literal translation of "plen an gwary" is "arena of the play" in the sense of drama, but the St Just arena is probably typical in having been the setting for "play" in the broader sense of contests of many sorts: wrestling, athletics, tests of strength and bravery - even duels, though perhaps they hardly come under the heading of "play". When William Borlase saw it in the 18th century it was still in good order, with six tiers of stone seating all round the central performing space, and was the obvious choice of venue for religious meetings: both the Wesley brothers preached here. A century later, though still occasionally used by visiting preachers and by miners for rock-drilling contests, it had degenerated into a town tip, and almost all trace of the seating had gone. Our own age has restored something of its old importance and function: plays have been performed there again, the Cornish Gorsedd ("meeting of bards") has assembled there - and it has even found a new rôle as a helicopter pad!

WALK 3
THE ST JUST MINES TRAIL
SECTION 3:
ST JUST, THE KENIDJACK
VALLEY (NORTH)
AND BOTALLACK MINE

About 5 miles.
Could be reduced to about 3.5 miles by omitting St Just,
in which case the best place to start would be at Botallack Mine.

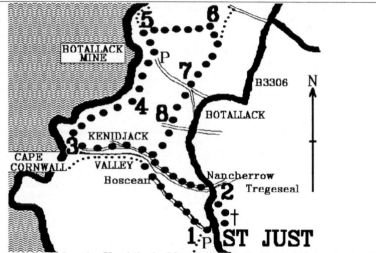

A walk that includes the Kenidjack (Nancherrow) Valley and Botallack will
scarcely need recommending to anyone with the slightest knowledge of
Cornish scenery and Cornish mining. Attempting to describe it has proved
a bit of a problem for me, simply because there is scarcely a square yard that
does not deserve comment, and I'm sure you could walk this route a
hundred times without noticing everything of historical interest. Much has
already been written about Botallack in particular, and there is no shadow
of doubt that a tremendous amount remains to be discovered. This is a
rather tougher walk than the previous one, with some steep climbs and the
likelihood of plenty of mud, especially on the field paths inland. To enjoy
the best of the cliff scenery you require a good head for heights, and dogs
and young children would need to be kept under strict control for their
own safety. You will not find any pubs, cafés, shops or public toilets along
the way unless you include St Just on the route, but the Queen's Arms in
Botallack village is only a few hundred yards from the clifftop part of
Botallack Mine: fork right after passing the farmhouse of Manor Farm.

Park in St Just, as directed for the previous two walks. Alternatively, park at Botallack Mine, which would give you the option of shortening the walk. For this, take either of the roads towards the coast from Botallack village, on the B3306 about a mile north of St Just. The roads meet and become a rough track leading to quite a large parking area on the right just past the Botallack count house, i.e. before you reach the prominent headgear at Allen's Shaft. (Trackside parking further on, which many drivers prefer if they want to admire the view without leaving their cars, is causing severe erosion, and therefore will be avoided by the kind of person I am writing this book for.) For this version of the walk, pick up the directions at point 4.

ST JUST CHURCH - AND ST JUST THE MAN

This grey, sturdy building may not be very different from many another old church in Cornwall, but it has a particularly strong appeal for me - largely, I suspect, because it seems so well suited to its setting within the hilltop town among the other bleak, windswept hills of its parish. The forthright plainness of its outside appearance is complemented by the ornate south porch that was added early in the 16th century, some 150 years after the bulk of the building was done. Inside, the church is a little disappointing, since it was thoroughly restored in 1865 according to the tastes of J. P. St Aubyn, who scraped off nearly all the plaster and replaced floor, roof, pews and glass. Luckily, a little old plaster was retained on the north wall, where parts of six medieval paintings had been hidden under whitewash ever since Henry VIII's decree of 1547 had required that all such "popery" be obliterated. The Victorian restorers considered two of them, "St George and the Dragon" and "Christ of the Trades", worthy of preservation. An interesting leaflet about the wall paintings is on sale in the church, together with a very full guide to the church as a whole. The latter draws attention to the beautiful 15th-century carvings on the sandstone piers, and tells of the discovery within the building in 1834 of the "Silus Stone", a headstone bearing the "Chi - Rho" Christian monogram and a Latin inscription. It is thought to date from the 5th century, and Charles Henderson in his *Cornish Church Guide* suggested that the inscription, "Selus ic iacit" ("Selus lies here"), "may prove to commemorate Selef, brother of St Just". Ian Cooke explores this possiblity in JTS. St Just or Iestyn and his brother were said to be sons or grandsons of the "king" or chieftain Gerent, otherwise known as St Geraint and as Sir Geraint in the Arthurian legends. His home was supposed to have been near Gerrans in the Roseland, so it is no surprise that the other two Cornish churches dedicted to St Just are nearby, at St Just in Roseland and Gorran Haven. Just and his brother, however, apparently wandered further west: Self, otherwise known as Seleven, lent his name to the parish of St Levan, and it was claimed in early times that Just was buried at "Lafrouda", now known as St Just in Penwith. The story is complicated by the fact that a man called Justus was created Archbishop of Canterbury in 616; John Buller in StJinP argued that the church was dedicated to him. All things considered, perhaps Oliver Padel's comment is better than all these rambling speculations: "almost nothing is known about the saint." (CPN)

1 Starting at St Just, turn right on leaving the car park (Market Street), and at Market Square continue ahead past the King's Arms towards the church (*). Take the footpath on the left beside the gate into the churchyard. Once you have passed the pretty granite cottages of Church Square the path is very obvious, running straight ahead and bringing you via four stiles down to the main road (B3306) at Tregeseal hamlet, opposite the attractive buildings of Nancherrow Farm. Cross the road with care, go a few yards to the right, over the bridge. On the opposite corner is the old toll house, now the Tregeseal Craft Shop, alias Bob Vigg's Gallery - a good place to buy original paintings and cards of the St Just area, as well as other local products.

2 Take the left turning, a narrow road leading down the Kenidjack or Nancherrow Valley. At the top is an impressive old barn, and a bob wall overlooks the road. This is what remains of the stamps engine house of Wheal Grouse, part of Wheal Owles, built by 1857 - possibly as early as 1830 - for a 30" engine. (There is a note about Wheal Owles later.) A pumping engine house once stood beside it, but only the base of that remains. Beyond the small sewage works, the valley begins to be dominated by a mine dump up on the right. Soon you will reach the short row of terraced cottages, described in <u>CAU</u> as almshouses, below the Wheal Drea engine house and the farm buildings of Kenidjack; up on the left is the small stack of Lower Boscean Mine. (See the note in Walk 2.) **(On the left here is the bridge by which those doing the full St Just Mines Trail join the route of this walk.)** Continue down the valley road, now little more than a track, keeping left where there is a fork. (A narrow path down to the left immediately after this - not a public right of way - leads to a little shed which houses a working waterwheel that drives a farm pump. It is good to know that the use of hydraulic power in this valley, where it was once so vital, has not altogether ceased.) Next come the picturesque and historically important ruins of the Kenidjack arsenic works: again see the note about Boscean Mine in Walk 2, and also the one about arsenic works later in this walk. The Kenidjack works appears to have treated arsenic from several local mines not big enough to have their own calciners. Still keep left, continuing beside the stream, and passing coast path signs left and right. The lower end of this valley (colour photo. 9) is one of my very favourite places, both for its beauty (especially in winter when the curse of Japanese knotweed is less obtrusive, the stream is in full spate, and the low sun casts dramatic shadows on Cape Cornwall and the craggy rocks closer at hand) and for the relics of Boswedden Mine (*) which lie all around. It's well worth crossing the stream if you can find a safe place to do so, because the huge wheelpit over there, built with dressed granite, is among the most impressive and best preserved in Cornwall. (Colour photo. 10) By the use of flat-rods, one of which passed through the small tunnel you will notice beside the stream, a 52-foot-diameter wheel there during the 1860s drove the pumps in two mineshafts, one upstream and the other nearer the sea. On the slope behind it is the ruined pit of a 30ft. wheel which drove "Water Whim", used for hauling skips in the Wheal Call diagonal shaft, now marked by a very large waste tip. The water that drove this wheel then passed over the larger one below. The ruined engine house among the dressing floors on the same (south) side contained a 28" beam engine for working the stamps and also for winding. Since so much water power was usually available here, steam engines did not often have to be used; even so, there was also a 37" or 40" one available for pumping, and the foundations of the house built for that are close to the track, on the right among the big spoil heaps. Both these engine houses were used by US Army engineers for demolition practice shortly before the Normandy landings. As you reach the rocks above the beach (Porthledden - say P'ledd'n), notice the remains of buddles; half of one of them has disappeared over the low cliff. Down by the beach a small building (now partly demolished) houses the ruins of a water turbine known as a Pelton wheel, probably installed by the hotel overlooking Cape Cornwall to supply electricity. There is a petrol engine there too, presumably for dry periods.

3 Next comes a stiff climb to the clifftop. You could go back up the valley-

An undated photograph, looking down the Kenidjack Valley. In the distance is the arsenic works stack, its cowl looking more secure than it does now; behind that are the rocks of Kenidjack Castle. The dryness of the stream may show that the picture was taken during a drought, but it could equally well indicate the large amount of water that was being taken out of it for the various dressing floors. The waterwheel in the foreground was probably driving a small battery of stamps protected by what looks like a flimsy roof on the far side. Up on the right is a revetted bank; presumably the ore for stamping was delivered from the top of that, using the steep chute. There is another waterwheel a few yards further downstream, powered by the tailrace from the upper one; again the gabled building may have housed stamps. It looks as if the tailrace from the second waterwheel was in turn conducted to a third, where there is yet another building which may have housed stamps. Just to the right of that building the superstructure of buddles is visible on the original photograph with the aid of a magnifying glass. To the right of the buddles is a calciner, perhaps the same one that appears in the August 1922 photograph. The same water was probably put to use at the arsenic works and yet more dressing floors in the lowest part of the valley.

track and take the signed coast path, but the best way, if you don't mind a scramble or two, is the first little path you come to (just beyond the engine house on the opposite side): this takes you across the dumps, where there are many interesting specimens of mineralised rock brought up by the miners, and you pass beside the base of the pumping engine house (notice the big mounting block for the balance bob) and, higher, a fenced shaft with a narrow entrance. Further up again, a small side path gives you the chance to peer out above Zawn Buzz and Gen, if you have the nerve for it. (Zawn is from the Cornish word for a cleft; the rest of the name is a mystery, to me at least.) During one of the breathers you will probably need to take as you continue upwards, look back to the opposite side of the valley: from here you can clearly see the various leats, similar to those on the same side of the Cot Valley (Walks 1 and 2). Most of them supplied the many waterwheels in the valley, but the highest continued right round to Cape Cornwall Mine to drive the stamps there. When you reach a wide track you need to go a few feet to the right and continue uphill on the signed coast path; but first you might be interested to look at the Kenidjack Quarries, around to the left. They were once linked to the B3306 by a tramway, parts of which can still be traced. These quarries were much in the news a few years back owing to the eviction from them of a group of travellers who had set up their distinctive little "bender" homes there. Local opinion mostly favoured the travellers against the authorities, and despite attempts to block access by means of huge

A tin-dressing mill employing two quite large waterwheels at Lower Boscean in the Kenidjack Valley. This was a little way upstream from the arsenic works, and you are looking up the valley, towards the site shown in the previous photograph. Up on the left is Kenidjack hamlet, with the engine house of Wheal Drea, part of Wheal Owles. The disaster that closed that mine occurred in 1893, just three years before the likely date of this photograph. In the foreground are at least three convex or "dumb" buddles.

BOSWEDDEN MINE

It is safe to assume that miners have exploited this area for many centuries, but records go back only to 1782. Several small copper-and-tin mines such as Wheal Call (or Caul or Cole), Great Weeth and Wheal Castle operated independently or in groups during the next fifty years, finally "consolidating" as Boswedden and Wheal Castle in 1836. In 1872 a larger group including also Boscean and Wheal Cunning was formed, by the name of Wheal Cunning United, but it was short-lived. The value of the Kenidjack / Tregeseal / Nancherrow / Boswedden stream (take your pick as to its name) for operating mills, both corn and stamping, was already fully exploited by the time the Rev. John Buller wrote about St Just (1840): "From this moor (Bostraze) flows a clear crystal stream of water, which maintains its purity, till it reaches the first mill in its winding course towards the sea. As it proceeds, it suspends a portion of the ochreous substance of the minerals, which are pounded and washed in numerous stamping mills to which it gives motion; till, by the time it reaches its destination, it becomes so turbid as to stain the sea ..." (StJinP) CAU estimates that the stream may have driven 50 waterwheels including those at the St Just Foundry. What was probably the largest waterwheel ever erected in Cornwall * - 65 feet in diameter - was in use at Wheal Call by 1837. The magnificent wheelpit that stands near the mouth of the valley now is not big enough to have contained it: that seems to have been built for a 30ft. wheel and to have been enlarged to accommodate a 52ft. wheel some time before 1865, which drove nearby buddles as well as operating pumps in two shafts by means of flat-rods. (To give you some idea of what such a wheel looked like, a drawing exists of the 54ft. wheel that was used at North Roskear Mine, near Camborne: see ECMH1, page 152.) By this time the mine was exploiting mineral lodes under the sea, had a work force of 155, and employed five steam engines, two of which operated only when conditions were too dry for the waterwheels. Rather surprisingly, perhaps, Boswedden was never very profitable, and its workings were closed down soon after the amalgamation with Wheal Cunning and Boscean. The flash flood that resulted from the thaw after the Great Freeze of 1892 destroyed many of the smaller mining structures that still remained in the valley; some of the larger ones were used for demolition practice during World War 2; and the rest would probably have vanished in recent years if Geevor's plans to rework the dumps had been realised.
*But it was modest compared with a few elsewhere. A 72ft. 6in. wheel was installed at Laxey Mine in the Isle of Man in 1854, and a vast 80ft. one was operating at a paper mill in Dublin ten years later. See ECMH1 for Barton's fascinating essay on "Water-engines in Cornish Mining".

boulders some of them were still living at Kenidjack early in 1993. At the clifftop a wooden stile enables you to cross a barbed-wire fence; then head for the coast-path post to the right of the ruined building. CAU suggests this may have been the quarry manager's house and quarry offices, but Kenneth Brown thinks it more likely to be associated with the rifle ranges mentioned below. Scattered all over this clifftop area are relics of many different periods and enterprises, some of them very hard to make sense of now. Beside the building is a small Early Bronze Age circle, at the centre of which was once a burial chamber; nearby are the ramparts of the Iron Age fortification known as Kenidjack Castle; a mine named after that, Wheal Castle, has left various fragments such as the base of an engine house and a small pond (now dry) which held water for its boiler; and the most substantial ruins, remains of the St Just Battery, which operated from about 1870 to the early 1900s. The firing positions and especially the butts (revetted with masonry, some of it taken from the engine house) are still clear to see. Although so little is left of the Wheal Castle engine house, something of its history is, I think, worth including here. It was built in 1883 for a rotative engine, about 22-in., "in connection with a short-lived reworking intended to open up an intersection between two important lodes under the sea a short way out from the cliff. The method used was remarkable. Instead of rehabilitating an old shaft ... above adit level, the skip road and pump rods were taken out and down the sheer face of the cliff! Then they entered the adit a short distance and were turned down the shaft which was enlarged to receive them. Fixing the installations, including a ladder road, down a

Possibly the last mining venture in the Kenidjack Valley: a little group of tin streamers photographed in August 1922. The building in the centre background housed a calciner, presumably part of the Kenidjack arsenic works. The men and boys were reworking dumps of material already processed at one of the old stamping mills, and it must indeed have been a matter of "eking out a livelihood", to quote the words of the person who gave this picture to the RIC. They had improvised a waterwheel by nailing seven-pound bully beef tins to a pony trap wheel. According to Clive Carter (quoted in <u>CAU</u>, top of page 45) this contraption operated one buddle and a set of stamps. The boys' wages were 7s 6d (37.5p) per week - 6d more than the usual wage in the district because the work was out of doors. When they reached sixteen years of age they were sacked to avoid payment of insurance by the employer.

windswept cliff with Atlantic breakers below is a feat which is better imagined than described!" (The quotation is from a set of notes provided by Kenneth Brown for one of his fascinating Trevithick Society field-trips.) As the path approaches Botallack Mine it runs beside an area which, early in 1993, was occupied by travellers living in ingeniously adapted old coaches; just past that point there is a choice of ways, both of which have much to offer as they pass through an area that is bewilderingly rich in remains of mining enterprises ancient and modern. To attempt to describe and explain everything would be to overload a book intended to be easily portable, and probably succeed only in confusing you, so I shall concentrate on the most prominent features. The first two are engine houses dating from about 1870, relics not of Botallack but of Wheal Owles (*). (Colour photo. 8) On the left is the stamps engine house of Cargodna and Wheal Edward (which became part of Wheal Owles), currently in imminent danger of collapse, so please do not risk going close to it until and unless it has been stabilised. This engine house was sited to draw from Cargodna shaft partway down the cliff using an upright axle cage on the seaward side of the house. It was from that shaft that the twenty doomed miners made their final trip into the workings on 10th January 1893. For many years, until it was removed by vandals, there was a plaque to the memory of the drowned miners on the collar of the shaft, which according to Dicon Nance is known as "consecrated shaft". All around the engine house are many features of considerable historical interest, including the footstep mounting of the upright axle steam whim, an incline shaft from which some pitchblende (uranium) was recovered, a tramway and an unusually large round buddle over 50 feet in diameter, but at present most of these are either wholly or partially hidden by vegetation and assorted rubbish. Some aspects of the design of the engine house suggest that there may have been a back bob to pump water for the dressing floors - compare the Narrow Shaft engine house which used to stand on the clifftop at Botallack. Fly-tipping also disfigures the second building, the Cargodna pumping engine house of Wheal Owles, whose shaft is choked with garbage. A 36" beam engine was installed to pump from it. Attached to the main building are the remains of its boiler house.

4 A little further along are 19th-century dressing floors of Botallack Mine (*), now very overgrown - you may be able to make out the remains of buddles. The tall stack marks one of the most impressive and in its way beautiful relics at Botallack, the arsenic works (*) built soon after the mine was re-opened in 1906: not even at Wheal Busy or Poldice are there such complete remains of a "lambreth". The building with a rather shapely arch a little below the flues housed a Brunton calciner (colour photo. 11); the power vault beneath it has been converted into a summer house ("Last of the Summer Wine"). Nearby are concrete dressing floors dating from the same period, with the massive foundations for Californian stamps above; all this was originally enclosed in a big mill building. Further up again, beside the pot-holed road leading inland, is the Botallack Count House, nicely restored and in use recently as a restaurant; alongside the parking space to the left of that some walls survive of the smith's shop, fitting shop, traction engine house, sawmill and men's dinner house - all built early this century, as was the tall chimney nearby. The modern headgear was erected in 1983 when the management at Geevor decided to re-open Allen's Shaft. The plan was to

WHEAL OWLES

As I write this - January 1993 - Wheal Owles (pronounced "Oals" or "Olds") is back in the news again. It is exactly a century since the mine was "knacked", following one of the worst mining disasters in a district that has known many. Like most if not all the other mines hereabouts, it consisted of a combination of many small old mines; for example, one called "Whele an Houl" ("the sun mine", perhaps, though "Owles" may derive from Cornish *als,* meaning cliff or shore) was at work by 1725. Wheals Edward, Drea, Grouse and Cargodna are perhaps the best known of them. The period of Wheal Owles' greatest prosperity was the 1860s, when it had 11 engines and "the staggering total of 29 miles of levels, 3 miles of adits, and an additional mile of levels being driven each year" (CAU). Poor prices for metallic ores during the '70s and '80s led to the closure of most of the inland sections of the mine; the best prospects seemed to be under the sea. In 1884 the decision was taken to focus all efforts on the Cargodna section, known by this time as West Wheal Owles, and the clifftop pumping engine there - described at the end of section 3 - was the only one that continued working. It was just before 9am on 10th January 1893 that miners broke through into the flooded 148 fathom level of Wheal Drea - which according to the plans they were relying on was nearly 40m away from where they were working. The torrent of water that surged through the new levels with a roar described by one of the survivors as "louder than ten thousand thunders" was so devastating that, according to CAU, it created enough air pressure to blow out a big crater near the Kenidjack almshouses. (Cyril Noall, however, mentions the belief that the hole resulted from the sudden outflow of water, "the unsupported ground then collapsing to adit level.") Some of the mine waste that still forms a large heap below the Wheal Drea engine house was later used to fill it. Nineteen men and a boy were drowned - their bodies have never been recovered - and the management soon gave up any attempt to drain the mine. Nearly ten pages of CMD are devoted to the Wheal Owles disaster; Noall gives a particularly vivid account of the bravery and practical intelligence of James "Farmer" Hall, who saved the lives of at least five men; and he includes many other memorable details, such as the sad paragraph about the young miner called Thomas who was due to be married that day. The wedding was postponed at the Vicar's request, and Thomas was among those who died. One miner, Thomas Lutey, had had forebodings of tragedy, and for several days beforehand had taken to running through the workings shouting "Water! Water!" In the event, Thomas and his brother Richard narrowly escaped with their lives, but Thomas never went underground again. He earned a meagre living selling oranges in and around St Just, "walking along the roads with a shuffling gait, his eyes always fixed on the ground, as if he were expecting the earth to open under his feet."
(If you want to understand the complex geography of the various lodes and shafts of Wheal Owles, the plan on pages 128-9 of CNSJ is useful, but note that the key is wrong: Nos. 7-12 should be given as 6-11.)

dewater it and clear away rubble down to 900 feet and then sink a new inclined shaft down to 2,000 feet to intersect with the Wheal Owles lodes under the sea. The 1985 crash in tin prices put paid to this scheme. A track leads down, past the site of Wheal Hazard Shaft, to the part of the mine that takes its name from the offshore islands, The Crowns, where still perch the most etched, drawn, painted and photographed engine houses in Cornwall (unless Wheal Coates, St Agnes, has that honour): the Crowns pumping-engine house, built for a 36" engine as far back as about 1835, and just above that the winding-engine house, built in 1862. The famous wooden skip-road shown in photographs of the royal visit of 1865 ran from that across the cliff face down into the new Boscawen Diagonal Shaft, which had been sunk to 225 fathoms (1350 feet) below the adit near the bottom of the cliff. The bottom of the shaft was under the sea, over half a mile from the shore. At this point you might find it helpful to refer to the 1850s engraving on page 1, showing the situation just before the Diagonal Shaft was sunk. The large headframe on the lower cliff-edge to the right was at Wheal Hazard Shaft; from that, overhead cables were carried up to a winding engine on the top which stood a little too far back from the edge to be visible in this view. The Crowns winding- / stamps-engine house is shown on the clifftop: some details about this are given later. Closest to the sea is the Crowns pumping-engine house, and just visible around the corner, half-way up the cliff, is the winding-engine house on Wheal Button Shaft. The gabled building underneath the Crowns whim may have housed mine offices or provided miners' accommodation.

Back on the main track at the top, notice the excavation on the inland side of the track, close to the coast path sign. Known as Grylls Bunny, it is a good example of "openwork", and may be a relic of some of the earliest mining in this area. The pit remains quite impressive despite the fact that material from Allen's Shaft was dumped in it during the 1980s, but the most interesting part of the Bunny is on the opposite side of the track, where several gunnises can be seen if you are prepared to scramble around on the rough little paths below. (Colour photo. 12) There is a "warren" of small chambers and tunnels, and this is thought by some to be the reason for the name, but the Cornish word "bonny", a bunch of ore, seems a more likely origin. (See StJP, page 17.) Not far past this, the coast path brings you to a small stack, all that remains - apart from a few foundations - of the Crowns whim engine house, built in 1841. The main job of this engine in the early years was presumably to raise ore to the clifftop from the various shafts below (probably including the Crowns Engine Shaft, although Kenneth Brown tells me there is no evidence of that), and a revetment wall on the edge of the cliff marks where the headframe for this purpose stood. (A horse whim had been used before 1841.) After the sinking of the Diagonal Shaft it drew skips up and down a long, steep timber incline leading to a loading bay near the top of the Diagonal Shaft's own skip road. A gully in the cliff face - not easily seen from the top - shows the course of the steeper skip road. The Crowns whim engine was also used to drive stamps, and at various periods it seems to have wound from Hazard Shaft and even from Wheal Cock, several hundred yards to the north. The dressing floors here were replaced by those served by the stamps engine on Narrow Shaft (roughly where the existing ruins of the arsenic works are), probably at about the time the Diagonal Shaft was abandoned in the mid-1870s.

5 Turn right beside the whim stack, following the coast path sign. **To continue the full St Just Mines Trail, turn left on the wide track (the coast path), picking up directions at point 3 in Walk 4.** For the rest of the 5-mile walk, go almost straight on, crossing the wide track; walk towards a farm gate, and take the path on the left just before that, where there is a metal bar to climb over or duck under. After a few yards between hedges, follow the hedge on your right, heading just right of a mine stack.

Despite the crack right across the glass plate negative, this photograph is worth including to illustrate the changes in the industrial landscape on the clifftop at Botallack. These eight men, with the possible exception of the one in the bowler hat, were conducting a survey in 1903. They were probably students from the Penzance School of Mines. Within the following ten years most of these buildings were swept away and replaced by a new arsenic works, a modern dressing plant including Californian stamps, and the headgear and buildings associated with a new shaft, Allen's. The stack on the left, however, looks like the one now at the end of the arsenic flue. The tall engine house was on Narrow Shaft, and contained an engine which hauled from the ·shaft on the far side as well as working stamps. The unusually high bob wall seen in the photograph supported a "back bob", a smaller beam attached to the main one. CAU states that the back bob powered the stamps, but another possibility is that it pumped water to the stamps from a "lobby" or reservoir. Mr Joff Bullen tells me this was the normal use to which back bobs were put in Cornish mines. The same engine house is seen in the distance on the next old photograph, and the two beams are clearly visible.

Where the hedge bends right, carry straight on to the field corner where there is a stile (beware of slippery stones). At the next field corner you have a rather steep, awkward "stile" to negotiate, which takes you up on top of a wall. After a few feet along that, cross the low stone stile on your left, and continue ahead towards the houses (Nineveh Farm), which you reach via a gate. The stack was originally part of a whim engine house, built in 1882 on the Carnyorth section of Botallack Mine. (Just why a farm in Cornwall should be named after an ancient Assyrian city I don't know. Sometimes such names are corruptions of Cornish words; for example, there are several Cornish farms called Ninnes or Ninnis, probably meaning remote, isolated spot.)

6 Almost opposite the farmhouse, cross the tumbledown stile on the right between two ruined buildings and walk with the hedge on your right. Cross the next stile and then go very slightly left to a third one at the corner; continue ahead with the hedge on your left to a fourth stile. **(Those doing the full St Just Mines Trail join the route here on the way back to St Just.)** Now the path goes slightly to the right via a low wall to another stile, straight on across a boggy patch to yet one more stile, and then along the farm lane ahead. Notice two old mineshafts on the left, surrounded by walls. At Manor Farm parts of the lane were very muddy in January, and we had to squeeze between obstructions presumably intended to stop cattle from straying on to the minor road beyond. The exterior of the pretty house on the right here, with tall chimneys - the farmhouse of Manor Farm - was used as "Nampara" in the first series of "Poldark" on television. It dates from 1663.

7 At the road junction turn right along a rough lane beside new bungalows, and continue along the path on the right side of a granite cottage (Parknoweth, if it hasn't been re-named). The path is clear, running between hedges. At the junction go a few yards to the right, and then left, uphill. This narrow lane between hedges runs up to a cottage beside a ruined engine house. This belonged to the original Wheal Owles and was built (before 1857, but the exact date is not known) for a 36" pumping engine. The shaft has been covered over by a car parking area.

8 At the T-junction go a few feet right, then left, along a path. After a stile the path runs between walls; then cross another stile and go straight across the field ahead. After two more stiles the track leads to the relatively well-preserved engine house on the left, which held a 26" engine used at first to hoist from Greenland's Shaft, the mouth of which is buried under the burrows in front of the house, and later to pump and perhaps also hoist from Wheal Drea Shaft, which is behind the house and at an angle. Kenneth Brown tells me that the stands for the flat-rods in the field behind the house used to be kept visible by pigs rooting. These shafts were both on the Wheal Drea section of Wheal Owles, the part that flooded after abandonment and brought about the 1893 tragedy. Continue straight on, down to the valley road, across the bridge ahead and up the track with the Lower Boscean stack on your left. Go left at the top, through Boscean hamlet, completing the route back into St Just as described at the end of Walk 2.

BOTALLACK MINE

When R. M. Ballantyne of *Coral Island* fame decided to base one of his boys' adventure novels on tin mining, the obvious choice for a setting was Botallack, "the most celebrated mine in the great county of Cornwall". In 1865, three years before Ballantyne published *Deep Down,* Thomas Spargo had claimed that "The Botallack mine is probably the most remarkable in the world .... a wonder, showing the enterprise of man, and his marvellous control over the earth on which he moves." (MC1) "One of the most singular combinations of the power of art and the sublimity of nature that can be imagined," declared Murray's Handbook of 1859 - and that was written before the days when the Boscawen Shaft brought such celebrity. Cyril Noall was clearly rather sceptical about a claim made by a mine manager in 1895 that Botallack had been worked for seven hundred years (CNB, page 150), but there is little doubt that the Botallack area, where the mineral lodes were exceptionally prominent in the cliffs, was among the earliest to be mined in the St Just district. John Norden (c.1584) wrote that the hamlet of "Botallock" was "moste visited with *Tinners,* where they lodge and feede, being nere their mynes," whereas his entries on Pendeen and St Just make no mention of mining. A large number of small independent enterprises (CAU lists almost 30 of them) combined under the name of Botallack - many of them by the end of the 18th century, some others not until the start of the 20th. At least one of the small mines, Wheal Cock, had already driven levels under the sea by 1778, when William Pryce wrote about the "thundering roar" of the Atlantic waves and the moving rocks on the sea bed heard by the miners below. "Add to this, that several parts of the Lode, which were richer than others, have been very indiscreetly hulked and worked within four feet of the sea; whereby, in violent stormy weather, the noise overhead has been so tremendous, that the workmen have many times deserted their labour under the greatest fear, lest the sea might break in upon them." (MC, p.21) For a colourful and humorous account showing how nerve-racking it was to be in that part of the mine even in calm weather, read Wilkie Collins' *Rambles Beyond Railways* (1851). Cyril Noall's history of Botallack shows how the foresight and determination of one man, Steven Harvey James, kept it alive during hard times in the late 1830s, when prices were low and most of the tin and copper from the shallower levels had already been recovered, and ushered in the period of its greatest prosperity. Its first royal visitor was Queen Victoria, in 1846. From the late '40s onwards it expanded steadily, taking over several neighbouring mines and venturing much further under the sea with the aid of the Boscawen Diagonal Shaft, begun in 1858, soon after the likely date of the engraving reproduced on page 1. Its name was a tribute to the owner of the mineral rights, Lord Falmouth. The descent of the new shaft by the Duke and Duchess of Cornwall (known elsewhere as the Prince and Princess of Wales) in 1865 went ahead despite a horrific accident in April 1863, when the chain attached to the iron gig broke as eight men and a boy were being hauled to the surface. This led to the substitution of wire rope for the chain: eventually chains were totally superseded by wire ropes throughout Cornwall and elsewhere. (Cyril Noall's *Cornish Mine Disasters* gives a long contemporary account in verse of "The Botallack Mine Tragedy", which includes the lines,

Young Peter Eddy's head was gone,
Upon the skip he lay,
The sollar struck him as they pass'd,
And took his head away.)

Botallack became one of the most fashionable "attractions" in Cornwall; the opening of the through-line between Paddington and Penzance less than two years after the royal visit increased the flow of visitors. They were, as Noall puts it, "not altogether welcome," since they took up the valuable time of mine officials and occupied places in the gig that might more profitably have been taken by miners, so a fee of half a guinea was charged, the proceeds to be given to miners' widows and those maimed through working there. After the '60s the mine's fortunes fluctuated, and problems caused by low prices or disappointing output were partly offset by sales of arsenic; but by the '90s so much cheap tin was being produced abroad that ruin was facing all Cornish mines, and when a cloudburst flooded the richest part of Botallack, Wheal Cock, in November 1894, followed by more underground flooding in February 1895, the mine's shareholders had no choice but to pay off the workforce and sell the surface plant. Eleven years later came an ambitious attempt to re-open the mine, and most of the remains on the clifftop date from this period. Unfortunately, the lease granted to the new company by Lord Falmouth stipulated that a new shaft - known as Allen's, after Francis Allen, one of the directors - had to be sunk at the point where the modern headgear now stands. This was a bad mistake, because the best prospects for rich new discoveries of ore lay well out to sea. For three-quarters of a century from 1914 Botallack was abandoned to the elements. In 1980 - the year when Botallack received its third royal visitor, Queen Elizabeth II - Geevor Mine decided to extend its workings into Botallack, and efforts were made to refurbish Allen's Shaft, but the crash in tin prices of 1985 prevented any underground development from taking place.

The best contemporary description of a visit to Botallack that I have read - and in fact it beats all accounts I have read of visits to any mine - is that by J. R. Leifchild (CMM, 1855). No brief extract can do it justice: get a copy! It was Leifchild who told the story of the Blind Miner of Botallack, who knew the underground workings so intimately "that he became a *guide to his fellow-labourers,* if by any accident their lights were extinguished!"

A large working model of the Crowns section of Botallack showing both of the skip-roads is the main exhibit at the small mining museum beside the Gem and Jewellery Workshop, Pendeen, which is on the south side of the B3306 - if you are approaching from St Just it is on the right, roughly half way between the Radjel Inn and the right turning to Penzance (B3318). I'm told that the model was made by an elderly retired miner. How accurate it is I don't know, but it gives a clearer impression of how that part of the mine operated than words, diagrams and photographs can.

This wonderful photograph of the Crowns section of Botallack is thought to date from the time of the royal visit, 1865, but I suspect it is rather later. On the right is the pumping engine house, built some 30 years before. The headgear attached to its bob wall stands over the Crowns Shaft. The other engine house nearby had only recently been erected. Its engine hauled wagons on the famous wooden skip-road which served the new Boscawen Diagonal Shaft. The very steep skip-road on the left close to the camera was operated from the top of the cliff, where there was a small whim engine house, of which only the stack now remains. The shed-like structure built across the Diagonal Shaft skip-road was the point where the ore from the Diagonal Shaft was transferred to the steep skip-road to be hauled to the clifftop. The capstan at the bottom-right-hand corner was for handling the "pitwork" (heavy equipment such as pump-rods) in Crowns Shaft. The engine houses on the clifftop in the distance are the Narrow Shaft winding/stamps building shown in the previous photograph (main bob on the left, back-bob on the right), built in 1860 and now almost totally gone; and on the right presumably the Cargodna pumping engine house of West Wheal Owles, built about 1870 - hence my suspicions that the photograph is later than 1865.

ARSENIC WORKS

Towards the end of the 19th century, when a combination of factors - principally foreign competition and the exhaustion of the shallower ore deposits which were the cheapest to mine - threatened the entire Cornish mining industry with extinction, a sudden increase in demand for arsenic offered some hope of at least postponing closure for the mines which had a good supply of it. It was during the 1870s that the value of arsenic as an insecticide began to be appreciated, especially in controlling Colorado beetles on potato plants and boll weevils on the cotton plantations of the USA. Other uses apart from its great convenience as a murder weapon were already known: these included cosmetics, tonics, sheep dips, soap for cleaning leather, the clarification of glass, and pigments, particularly a brilliant green much used in Victorian wallpapers which became notorious when acidic pollution in city air reacted with it to produce deadly arsene gas. (The theory that the arsenic in Napoleon's wallpaper on St Helena hastened his death has been dismissed by at least one expert.) Until the early 19th century, the arsenic content of ore was regarded as a menace because it spoilt the tin for smelting, so the stamped ore was roasted in "burning houses" and the noxious substances given off (sulphur as well as arsenic) were consigned to the atmosphere where they could do no harm. In order to collect the arsenic, basically all that was needed was to attach a very long flue to the furnace (known as a "calciner", pronounced "cal-sign-er") with a tall chimney at the end to provide a strong draught. As the gases cooled the arsenic condensed and formed crystals on the walls of the flue. When sufficient had collected, the calciner was stopped, iron doors in the flue were opened, and the arsenic "soot" was swept or shovelled out. To gain the maximum length of flue within a limited space, it was usually built in a zig-zag form, known as a labyrinth ("lambreth" in Cornwall). Finally the "soot" had to be treated at a refinery. 1812 saw the first attempt to produce arsenic commercially, when an old smelting works at Perranarworthal, south of Truro, was converted into a refinery. The growth of the industry is charted in some detail in ECMH2; see also my own *Book of the Poldice Valley.* During the 1830s an improved type of calciner invented by William Brunton was introduced which rotated automatically, ensuring that the ore was roasted evenly. The improvement in the market for arsenic 40 years later spawned several arsenic works around St Just. The *Cornish Telegraph* of 1st September 1875, for example, reported that "Botallack has no end of arsenic on the surface and underground. ... Now that £6 10s. a ton can be obtained for it, the old burrows and reserves are being hunted. ... Half a dozen circular kilns ... are being built. ... A cross-flue leads inland to the main flues - a series of arched chambers, 72 in number ... then a stack, 112 feet high, conducts the smoke ... to the upper air." The works in the Kenidjack Valley may be rather earlier, to judge by the fact that it used old-fashioned condensing chambers rather than lambreths. Although the arsenic trade declined during the 1880s there were revivals later, for example in 1906-9 (the impressive arsenic flues at Botallack date from that period: the older ones seem to have left little trace), and during World War I, when according to Bryan Earl the need for poison gas caused the price of arsenic to rise from £9 a ton to over £100. (*Journal of the Trevithick Society,* 1983)

WALK 4
THE ST JUST MINES TRAIL
SECTION 4:
LEVANT, GEEVOR AND
BOTALLACK

About 4 miles

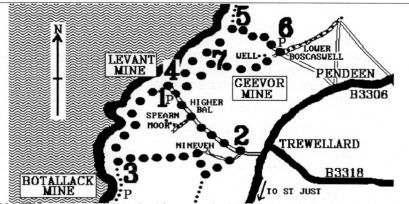

NOTES: *(1) Although this route includes part of the area mined by Botallack, the most famous remains of Botallack Mine are visited in Walk 3.*
(2) If you are doing Walk 4 as part of the St Just Mines Trail, you need to pick up the directions at point 2, line 13.
(3) This is a figure-of-8 walk, so could easily be shortened or done as two separate walks of about 2.5 miles (southern part) and 1.5 (Geevor). For the latter, start at point 4.

As this is a rather short walk, it allows time for a visit to the restored Levant engine, and perhaps also to the Geevor mine buildings and museum. I say "perhaps" because I suspect that the Geevor site will require several hours or even a full day to do it anything like justice, especially if a visit to the shallower underground levels that remain above the water line is included. Some information about opening times at Levant is given at the end of the note about that mine; for up-to-date details contact the National Trust. The walk itself is another splendid one, as much for the awe-inspiring cliffs as the mining remains. Since the latter include some that date from very recent years, the route passes through one quite large area of modern industrial plant surrounded by derelict or semi-derelict land which is far from being a thing of beauty, but even this could perhaps be a joy for ever if the much-publicised plans to develop Geevor into a "visitor centre" are realised. The walk is an easy one, involving no steep gradients, but mud may cause problems on the inland field paths. Once again, there are no "facilities" such as toilets or pubs along the way, although the Trewellard Hotel is on the B3306 not too far from point 2 in the directions. I presume refreshments will be available at Geevor if and when it re-opens for visits.

There is a convenient car park at Levant Mine, which is at the coastal end of a rather rough and narrow road leaving the B3306 at Trewellard, beside a large chapel. Early in 1993 there was a small sign, Levant Engine, at the point where you need to turn - about a quarter of a mile after the main entrance to Geevor Mine if you are approaching from the St Ives direction.

1 Begin by returning along the road to Trewellard, known as Levant Road. Soon you reach what looks like a younger brother of the ramparts of the Plymouth barbican or a fortification designed by Vauban. This massive wall includes two chutes which enabled ore to be loaded on to wagons, and a flight of steps leads up to what a lady we met nearby told us local people call Arabelle: one of the best-preserved of all the engine houses in the St Just area. It (or perhaps I should say "she") was built in 1887 for a 35" engine used for pumping and winding in the Guide Shaft of Levant Mine (Higher Bal). Part of the boiler house has survived, and it is easy to see where its lean-to roof was attached to the main building. Because of the two jobs the engine had to do, the structures (loadings) between the engine house and its concrete-capped shaft are unusually complex. They are interpreted in detail in CAU, and perhaps in due course, if and when public rights of access to this site are formalised, some kind of explanatory notice will be provided. Meanwhile, the photograph on page 15 of LCCM is a useful guide; it certainly shows very clearly why that great wall was needed, to retain the huge pile of waste. Continue towards Trewellard.

The first right turning, a wide track or dirt road heading towards the Allen's Shaft headgear at Botallack, offers the chance of a short diversion to see the scanty but still rather impressive remains of a stamps-engine house that belonged to Spearn Moor Mine, part of Spearn Consols, surrounded by the ruins of dressing-floor buildings. To find it, turn right again, towards the coast, and cross the stile. The Spearn mines, not among the most successful, produced mainly tin, and were eventually amalgamated with Levant. This engine house was built by 1878 for a 30" engine. A photograph showing the building as it was in 1951 is in CEH (page 12). The Higher Bal engine house is also seen in the background. Return the same way - or you could greatly shorten the walk by continuing to the cliffs.

2 Before you reach the edge of Trewellard, notice on the right, a couple of hundred yards away among fields, the exceptionally small whim-engine house of Spearn Moor Mine, built for a 20" engine. It is probably over 150 years old, and therefore one of the earliest surviving engine houses in the district. There were large dumps of waste beside it till the early 1980s, when they were scooped up and put through the Geevor mill for tin recovery. Take the road on the right immediately before the first building on that side. The road soon becomes a rough track between hedges, which turns right after about a hundred yards. At that point the track apparently ceases being a right of way, so cross the granite-block stile on your left, and after a few yards beside a wooden fence cross the small wooden stile ahead and walk with the low hedge on your right. The next stile, a stone one, is straight ahead, and after some fifty yards there's another on your right (steps down). After that, continue in the same direction across a field to a stile in the far corner. **Now if you are doing the full St Just Mines Trail continue ahead,**

following the directions starting part-way through point 6 in Walk 3. To continue Walk 4, cut back sharply to your right at this point, over a stile and across the field beyond to another stile, then beside a hedge and over two more stiles to Nineveh Farm. There turn left, go through a metal farm gate and follow the clear path heading towards the modern headgear at Allen's Shaft, Botallack. The small stack on your left is commented on briefly in section 5 of Walk 3. After the gap in the hedge, keep beside the hedge on your left, cross the stile on your left at the corner and walk a few feet along a wall going to the right, close to an old pump. After the rather steep and awkward descent from the wall, keep by the hedge on your left again, cross a stile (slippery in moist weather), and go straight across the next field, heading very slightly left of the houses. After a short distance beside a hedge on your left, go along the path between hedges to your left.

3 Turn right on the dirt road; this is, in fact, the coast path. From here northwards for a mile or so the coast path runs well inland, and if you keep to it you will miss some stupendous cliff scenery as well as some interesting and even breathtaking mining relics. Almost immediately on your left you will notice a small stone bridge with its arched opening blocked. The mines depended on a constant supply of clean water for their dressing floors and engines (whether these were powered by steam or by waterwheels), and the miners skilfully and laboriously used to the full every drop available, creating reservoirs and building leats, sometimes several miles long. This particular leat, though dry now, can easily be followed as it runs north west towards the cliff edge through old dressing floors near the white trig. point marker close to Botallack Head. This area was worked by Wheal Cock, which was already extracting copper and tin beneath the sea by 1778, taking over even earlier small enterprises with names including Wheal Hen and Wheal Chicken, and which itself became part of Botallack after 1842. Much of the clifftop here is covered with mine waste - residue from the dressing of copper ore - and there is a large number of ruined buildings, foundations, masonry walls and so on, reflecting the complex history of this mine over two or more centuries.

If as you walk on you keep fairly near the cliff edge you will soon overlook one of the most awe-inspiring places I know, Wheal Cock Zawn and, just beyond it, Stamps and Jowl Zawn, easily recognisable by the natural arch on the far side of the wider inlet beyond, through which the sea was pounding and foaming on the second day of 1993. Its name is apt (Cornish, *stampes an dyowl sawn,* "The Devil Stamps Gully" - "stamps", of course, referring to Cornish stamps machines): beautiful though it is, the scenery might indeed be a fit home for the devil, and somehow its fearsomeness is redoubled by the evidence that men have delved into these rocks and under that sea. The mine's main shaft was close to the cliff edge at Wheal Cock Zawn, and a house for a 24" pumping engine stood beside it; Skip Shaft is higher up the cliff, and a 16" winding-engine house was provided for that. The pumping engine house and the tall headgear on the clifftop, half-hidden by a large burrow, are well shown on the photograph on page 137 of <u>CNB</u>. When Wheal Cock was reworked early this century the stone from the pumping-engine house and other mine buildings such as the miners' dry, a smithy and stores, was used to build the massive retaining wall on the slope between the shafts plus linings inside the mouths of both shafts and walls around them. (See photograph 10 in <u>MIC</u>.) In January 1993 these mouths were being fitted with welded steel grills.

A rusty but still strangely impressive sculpture of a fantasy cockerel has been set up to overlook the zawn that bears its name. (A few days after I had written that, the sculpture was featured on local TV. To my surprise, the sculptor, Tom Leaper, made no reference to cocks: his work is punningly called The Flight of Cornish Industry. It was constructed quite recently from bits of a BMW car that was driven over the cliff in 1985 or '6, and Mr Leaper's original plan was to portray a spider. He has to come here regularly to repair it following the ravages of harsh weather and "determined vandals".)

The Pathfinder map indicates a waterfall at Stamps and Jowl. This was not visible to us (perhaps it is best seen from out at sea, or from the nearby headlands); but the two springs feeding the stream running to the cliff edge. were easy enough to find, and beside one of them is part of a low wall, the remains of a small dam. This water was evidently needed at Levant mine,

Levant photographed in about 1923 by Jack Trounson: that's his bike! From left to right : the whim engine house at Skip Shaft, with low stack; the calciner stack further away on the clifftop; the pumping engine house with small headframe, and its detached stack further right; in the distance the stamps engine house, linked to the skip shaft by an inclined tramway; the count house, with the smithy behind it; the small round explosives magazine in the foreground; and on the far right the compressor house. The miners' dry and the shaft and engine house for the man engine were further right, not in view here. On the original photograph it is just possible to discern the lighthouse on the headland.

LEVANT MINE

"A shock, sudden and riveting, met my eyes on the next headland.
"From the edge of the cliff stretching inland and westward along the coast every spot of green has long been uprooted. Over all that headland was the ugly paraphernalia of an ancient mine in full working order. The sea at the base of the cliff is dyed red, the surface of the hill is rent and scarred, heaped high with rubbish, and from dingy chimneys black smoke issues. I heard the pounding of stamps, saw the conduits, the various receptacles where the tin is washed, and the ever-running discoloured water. This is the famous Levant Mine, whose working run for a mile or more under the sea." (C. Lewis Hind: *Days in Cornwall,* 1907)
"If any one mine in West Cornwall could be said to summarise this ancient industry, it must be Levant." (Kenneth Brown, writing in <u>LCCM</u>.) This was the greatest of all the St Just Mines (unless Geevor takes that honour by virtue of its production in our own century), and it has probably had more written about it than any other mine in Cornwall. Despite all that, its name remains a mystery. Its literal meaning, "rising" (hence the east, land of the rising sun), could perhaps have been chosen for its optimistic implications, like so many other Cornish mine names. Cyril Noall tentatively suggested that it might refer to the Levant Company, which traded - partly in tin - in the eastern Mediterranean towards the end of the Tudor period (<u>CNG</u>). If he is right, the antiquity of mining here seems to be indicated; but the earliest known reference to such mining dates from 1670, and the earliest use of the name Levant is in 1748. Levant Mine proper was launched in 1820, and its career was to last 110 years. The total value of the minerals it produced has been estimated as more than £2.25m. at contemporary values, thus placing it within Cornish mining's "top ten". Its output was mainly copper till the 1850s, but tin predominated after that. Although the Great Depression of the 1930s forced Levant to close at long last, its ore deposits - especially those far out under the sea - were still proving productive right up to 1991 as part of the expanded Geevor. Reading a book like *The Mine under the Sea,* written by a miner who began his working life in 1917 as a boy of 14, you cannot help noticing a sense of pride in having been part of "the Levant", as he calls it, and even a kind of affection for the old mine, in spite - or maybe even because - of the fact that the management was more reluctant than most to move with the times. Some innovations had, of course, been inevitable, since the workings extended an unprecedented distance under the sea bed, resulting in equally unprecedented problems. There were two vertical shafts connecting underwater levels, and it was necessary to haul ore up them. Almost unbelievably, in 1886 a steam whim engine and boiler were set up in a specially excavated cavern at the top of Old Submarine Shaft, 210 fathoms below adit, and "It worked despite the heat and smoke," says John Corin. A visitor the following year reported that the temperature there was usually 100°F. Compressed air, which had been in use for drilling since 1880, was a much better alternative: New Submarine Shaft was equipped with a compressed-air winding engine in 1897, and in 1901 the company invested heavily in a horizontal triple-expansion engine complete with flywheel weighing 20 tons, installed in the Power House referred to in section 7 of the directions. The availablity of high-pressure

air in the further reaches of the mine helped to make working conditions more tolerable. (Jack Penhale describes a place nicknamed "Little Hell" where the men "had to have a compressed air supply to make ventilation and to lower the temperature by a degree or two.") Little concern for working conditions was shown, however, when the management decided in 1891 to use a steam locomotive for tramming wagons underground, and when they abandoned this experiment this was nothing to do with the noise, heat and stench but because the weak, sharply-curving track and damp conditions created problems. A pit pony was tried instead, with such success that a team of seven ponies came into use - the only known example of ponies working underground in Cornwall before World War I. An innovation which did prove beneficial to all was the telephone system, installed in 1895. In many other respects, though, the management's preference was to stick to time-honoured methods and keep the old machinery going as long as possible; and I suppose it could truthfully be said that the two things for which Levant is best known today both result from that attitude. The man engine had undoubtedly been a great boon to the miners for many decades, but Levant persisted in using its man engine long after all the others in the county had been abandoned or superseded. Hindsight is, of course, very helpful in achieving wisdom, but it seems clear now that the horrific disaster of 20th October 1919, 62 years after the machinery had been installed, was "just waiting to happen". Exactly what did happen and why is fully explained in many other publications, notably CNL and LCCM, but once again I would particularly recommend Jack Penhale's little book, which begins with a graphic description of his first ride on the man engine and ends with his own narrow escape on what he calls "D-Day": "D for Death, D for destruction, D for destiny". Another piece of machinery that had a long life was a 24" (later enlarged to 27")-cylinder steam engine made in about 1840 by Harvey's of Hayle and used to haul skips in a shaft on the cliff edge overlooking Levant Zawn. 90 years later it was still at work. Five years after the mine's closure it was saved from being scrapped, largely through the actions of J. H. Trounson. The Cornish Engines Preservation Committee was formed, and managed to raise enough money to buy it. It is now the oldest surviving beam engine in Cornwall. The Committee founded what is now called the Trevithick Society. Since 1966 the Levant Whim Engine has belonged to the National Trust, but the Trevithick Society is still very actively involved. An entertaining series of articles by the self-styled "Greaser-in-Chief", Milton Thomas, has been appearing in all recent issues of the Trevithick Society Newsletter, detailing the work in progress to restore the old engine and associated equipment and buildings. Whenever I visit, either Milton himself or another of his team always seems to be there, hard at work but ever ready to answer questions and show people around, if time allows. The original plan to have the engine back in steam to celebrate its 150th birthday proved over-ambitious; instead, the great day is to be Good Friday 1993. Following that the plan is for the engine to be in steam and open to the public from 11 am to 4 pm on the following days:
Until the end of May: Fridays and Bank Holiday Sundays & Mondays
June: Every Friday and Sunday
July to 19th September: Daily except Saturdays.

nearly a mile away, so a leat was constructed to carry it along the cliff. The leat (dry now, like the earlier one - but I believe there is a plan to bring it back into use again one day) is very easy to follow for most of its length, and being very level (except where the water had to be carried across small gullies by means of a launder hung on chains), it makes an ideal footpath. (Colour photos. 13 & 14) Just above the natural arch and below Carn Vellan there is a small rock stack, and it appears that the miners blasted out a cleft behind that for the leat to pass through. The leat path gives a fine view of the far side of the arch, and later of several shafts. As you approach the mine buildings at Levant (*) a strand of barbed wire warns you that you need to veer a little to the right because the last few yards near the cliff edge above Boscregan Zawn are too dangerous to walk along. The water served the whim and pumping engines (the cooling pond beside the restored whim engine has been reinstated, and - as I hinted earlier - there are hopes that one day the water in it will be supplied from its original source), but it seems that some of it was also carried further north-east, probably to a waterwheel at old dressing floors.

4 A visit to the refurbished whim engine house, if and when it is open, is not to be missed. Even if you cannot go inside to see the engine and boiler, it's worth walking around the sea-side of the building, past the pond just mentioned. Peer down over the retaining wall (can you work out how it was built?) and you will see the tortuous path down to the adit mouth not far above high-water level in Levant Zawn. Until it collapsed some forty years ago, there was a spectacular bridge from the end of the path, along the west side of the zawn and into the adit. This was the normal method of entering the underground workings before the installation of the man engine - of which more later. Behind you, under the small headgear erected in recent years by Geevor, is the 278-fathom-deep Skip Shaft, in which skips were raised and lowered by the whim engine. (The answer to my quiz question a few lines back, by the way, is as follows: the cliff-edge was cut back to form a "plat" a few feet wide at the base of the intended wall, the building stone was lowered down to that, and the builders perched on the top of the wall as they built it. No need for safety nets, scaffolding or anything like that! The wall has recently been re-pointed by the volunteers restoring the Levant engine - all part of the service .... All this and much more my wife and I were told during our last visit by one of the members of the Levant "gang", many of whom are mines - if you'll pardon the term - of colourful information about the history of Levant and the restoration work being carried out.) The tall ruined engine house is a very early one, built in 1835 for Levant's pumping engine, originally 40", later 45". The pumping shaft or Engine Shaft as it is usually called, now covered with a flat-roofed building, is very close to Skip Shaft but entirely separate. In recent years it was used to provide ventilation in the Geevor workings, and the building contains a fan for that purpose; the fan no longer operates, but steam often issues through the small gauze "roof", because the rock below is very hot. The rails a little further along are modern; the original tramway by which the ore raised in Skip Shaft was taken to the stamps ran in a tunnel (now blocked) under this area, and up the still visible incline. Workshops once stood on the concrete base beside the tramway. Continue along to the blackened stack near the cliff edge, noticing the slight signs of the leat, as mentioned at the end of point 3. The flue on the far side

. At the seaward end of the Nanquidno valley (Walk 1). The waste heap of rounded stones beside the Nanjulian stream provides clear evidence of tin streaming.

. Winter colours at the mouth of the Cot Valley (Walk 1). Notice the many heaps of mine waste on the far side. On the skyline is the stack of the whim-engine house of Bosorne and Ballowall Mine.

5. *The stack of the whim-engine house of Bosorne and Ballowall Mine, with Land's End in the distance (Walk 2) (31.12.92).*

6. *This photograph of the same stack was taken about five minutes earlier than No. 5. In the foreground is part of the Ballowall Barrow (Walk 2).*

9. Winter colours in the Kenidjack Valley, with Cape Cornwall in the distance (Walk 3) (1.1.93).

10. Boswedden Mine, Kenidjack Valley (Walk 3): the magnificent wheelpit of dressed granite. Just visible in the top-left corner are the remains of the smaller wheelpit which housed "Water Whim". This hauled from Wheal Call diagonal shaft, the mouth of which lies buried under the burrow to the right.

11. Botallack Mine (Walk 3): the Crowns engine houses as seen from the ruins of the Brunton calciner on the clifftop.

12. Part of the cliff workings at Botallack known as Grylls Bunny (Walk 3).

13 & 14. *The leat that supplied water to Levant (Walk 4). In the distance can be seen Pendeen lighthouse (left), and the main surviving buildings at Levant.*

15. Boscaswell Holy Well (Walk 4; also close to Walk 5).

16. The cliffs immediately below Geevor Mine. The ruined buildings are mostly the remains of Levant's dressing floors (Walk 5).

17. The confluence of the Rose and Portheras streams (Walk 5). Near the top of the picture can be seen the course of at least one of the leats by which the dressing floors in the Portheras Valley were supplied with water from the Rose stream.

18. One of several ruined tinworks higher up the Portheras Valley (Walk 5).

19. Morvah Consols: the ruined engine house, with Carn Galver in the distance (Walk 5).

20. Morvah Consols: part of the extensive ruins of the dressing floors.

21. Part of the tinworks in the Porthmeor Valley (Walk 6).

22. Porthmoina Valley: part of an old grist mill, later adapted to house Cornish stamps (Walk 6).

23. The altar stone in Madron Chapel or Baptistry (Walk 7).

25. The upper wheelpit at Carnelloe, with Gurnard's Head beyond (Walk 8).

24. Gurnard's Head Mine (Walk 8). The remains of the stack on the right, with Treen Cove beyond, and Carnelloe Point in the distance.

26. The remains of "Chapel Jane", on the cliff edge west of Gurnard's Head (Walk 8). In the middle distance can be seen the lower wheelpit

28. Rosevale Mine: some of the authentic equipment beside the mouth of the lower level (Walk 8). In the distance, a glimpse of Zennor church.

29. The lonely ruins of the Trevega Bal stamps-engine house (Walk 9). The truncated remains of the pumping-engine house - not visible at this distance - are about half-way down the slope on the far side of Brea Cove.

30. Hor Mine: the tumbled masonry wall on the edge of a wide shaft is all that remains of its engine house (Walk 9).

31. Approaching Carn Galver at the end of Walk 6.

of the stack suggests this was where arsenic was extracted from the ore; remains of calciners some distance to the north-west confirm this. After passing some ruined buddles you come back to the coast path, and here you are entering the area now associated with Geevor Mine (*), where there is a complex mixture of old and new mining relics, including batteries of rectangular settling tanks and huge mounds of waste material. Walk on beyond the small old stack on the right.

5 For the full St Just Mines Trail, continue on the coast path, picking up the directions near the start of point 2 in Walk 5. To visit Geevor and/or complete Walk 4, take the inland path which passes a small pond (presumably a miniature tailings dam) and crosses a stream by means of a wooden footbridge. After this the narrow path goes uphill; beyond a wooden stile it turns left and right; then it continues as a wider grassy track with a hedge on the left and brings you to the houses of Lower Boscaswell. (About fifty yards down the track on the left here are the remains of a fogou, but it is on private land, surrounded by barbed wire and rubbish, and sadly neglected. A hoard of about a hundred Roman copper coins was unearthed quite close to the fogou early in the 18th century.) Continue ahead through the village, with its attractive old cottages, their gardens surrounded by tall stone walls.

6 Soon after passing a small converted chapel (or school?), now deprived of its bell, you reach an open space where several roads meet. Here turn right along a track, past a long bungalow named (in 1993) Wheal Zandra. Soon you need to fork left to enter the main Geevor Mine site, but first you might care to find the Boscaswell Holy Well (colour photo. 15), which is just round to the right beyond the last bungalow. A. Lane-Davies says it is known locally as the Hesken ("sedge") Well, and an old lady told him it was "noted for horse leeches which .... were frequently caught for medicinal use on cattle as well as human beings. .... They would never bite any but a diseased part. She spoke as if they knew the difference." (HWC) See HWCCC for a detailed description of the well. Continue through the gate to the mine now. Early in 1993 a sign forbade entry "unless accompanied by official guide". This is, however, a public footpath according to the Pathfinder map, and now that the mine is closed it is clearly being used as such again. Presumably the plans to convert Geevor into a visitor centre will include proper signposting of rights of way through the site. Until then, I suggest you walk straight ahead, passing close to the tall headgear at Victory Shaft, and then turn right down a wide road towards the coast. There is a narrow footpath on the left after a short distance, but this looked overgrown and unusable; if reopened it will probably be the best way back to Levant. Till then, you will need to go on down the main roadway and thread your way among the modern waste-tips. You will eventually come to a broad stony track, which is the coast path.

7 Turn left on this, uphill. You pass a group of at least five old buddles before reaching a stack with the remains of an engine house close by - little more than its foundations now. This was built about 1845 for a 36" engine, mainly to work the stamps on Levant mine, though it also pumped water from a nearby shaft for use on the dressing floors. Follow the coast path sign to pass on the right of a second stack (notice the decorative brickwork, typical of several of Levant's chimneys). The ruins of Levant's Power House are still

GEEVOR MINE

Allen Buckley in <u>GM</u> mentions several small mines and tin streams working in the Geevor area which registered their names as early as the 1490s. A mine called While an Giver (possibly "mine of the goat(s)"), recorded in 1716, and again in 1765 with the slightly changed name of Wheal Geavor, was just one of many small ventures exploiting the area north of the much more important Levant. It was not till 1851 that a successful attempt to amalgamate these mines took place, and the new company called itself North Levant - hoping, no doubt, to attract investors by using that magical word. The mine proved to be moderately successful, and although low prices forced closure in 1891 it was reopened the following year, this time by the name of Wheal Geevor. Over the next 20 years there were several stops and starts and further changes of name, but 1911 saw the creation of Geevor Tin Mines Ltd and was the start of a long period of steady expansion and modernisation. The mine's main shaft, named after Oliver Wethered, a Director at Geevor since 1904, was near the main entrance to the site, but work on a vital new shaft further west was begun in 1919, named Victory in honour of the Allies' triumph the previous year. By the end of the '50s most of the tin in the Geevor sett had been mined, and all the adjoining workings were flooded; Geevor, as Cyril Noall put it, had to "break through the watery barriers." It was clear that the best prospects lay under the sea. In the late '60s came the considerable feat of plugging the breach by which the sea had entered the "40 backs" at Levant, where stoping above the 40-fathom level a century or more before had brought the workings dangerously close to the sea bed. At a notoriously weak spot, sea water had constantly trickled through, but no major breach had occurred by the time the mine closed in 1930. It seems likely that the later break-through resulted from the pressure of flood water inside the workings after the pumps ceased operating. The task of sealing the breach took five years to complete and involved the use of many thousands of tons of concrete. Fifty million gallons of water were then pumped out in the process of draining the Levant workings to a depth of 190 fathoms. In the event, the prospects uncovered in Levant were disappointing and the old mine was never unwatered to the bottom again. At about the same time, Geevor was finding excellent deposits of tin in a previously untouched lode to the north-east, in an area formerly worked by Boscaswell Downs Mine. In 1975 Victory Shaft was extended deep under the sea by means of a "sub-decline", that is, an incline shaft 15 feet wide and 10 feet high which began at the 15 level, some 1,500 feet below surface, and went beneath the old Levant levels. In 1980 work started on refurbishing Allen's Shaft at Botallack, with the aim of exploring in depth the inland portion of the lodes between Victory and Allen's Shafts. By the mid-1980s the mine had reached a depth of 2,200 feet and there were more than 100 miles of tunnels. The catastrophic fall in tin prices in 1985 dashed hopes of a bright future for Geevor, which shut down the following April. The pumps were kept going, however, and production resumed in 1987. This was achieved partly by exploiting the "tourist attraction" potential of the mine: to complement the mining museum founded in 1977, the company offered conducted tours of the surface plant and underground visits. (I am the proud possessor of a document bearing the logo of "Gever the Goat" and proclaiming, "This is to certify that Bob Acton has been down the mine and under the sea," signed by our guide, Allen Buckley. A memorable experience it was, too. Incidentally, Mr Buckley's little book on Geevor is rather hard to find now, but will I hope be available again one day at the Geevor Museum, and perhaps elsewhere. As well as giving a clear and interesting outline of the mine's history, he tells some memorable stories of heroism and hair's-breadth escapes. One concerns a miner, Jimmy Sedgeman, who used his pick to try to stop a rock that started moving towards him, but the weight of the stone pinned him to the wall and drove the wooden hilt of the pick right through his chest. The hospital staff, though "dumbfounded by the sight", operated so successfully that Jimmy made almost a complete recovery.) Despite the success of the tourism venture, the company had to lay off 122 employees and "put the mine back into mothballs" in February 1990, and it finally surrendered to the apparently inevitable towards the end of 1991: the pumps were switched off. In October of the same year the *West Briton* announced that "Cornwall County Council has given the go-ahead for a leisure plan to turn Geevor tin mine into a leading tourist attraction," and that "a full feasibility study" was already being prepared. A year later the purchase of the site by Cornwall County Council was announced; an ambitious scheme for "a quality museum" which would "generate wealth in the area" was described by the Council's countryside officer, but another official ominously warned that "the scale of the task is enormous and in the present financial situation there will be no instant solution." (*West Briton,* 8.10.92) Legal problems exist regarding ownership of the site, and much of the surface plant has now been ripped out by scrap merchants, but Stuart Smith of the Trevithick Trust remains confident of Geevor's great potential as an "interpretative centre" for Cornish mining. As I was writing this book early in 1993, preparations were under way under the auspices of the Trust - much of the work being done by ex-miners - for a planned opening early in the summer, with the mining museum and tours of the surface plant available from the start, and hopes that underground visits above adit level would be possible a year later.

attached to it, despite stone-robbing and the best efforts of the graffiti artists. It was built in 1901 for an air compressor, a huge steam engine which filled the whole building, said to have been the largest engine Holman Bros. of Camborne ever made. In 1919 electric compressors replaced it. Just before you reach the main track or road you will find the long concrete floor of what was once the miners' dry, a wooden building erected in 1889, said to have provided some of the best facilities on any Cornish mine. (See photo 22 in MC1.) At least two baths are still clear to see. A circular stairway in the dry led down to a short tunnel passing under the road to the man-engine shaft: by using this the miners could avoid exposure to the elements on entering or leaving the shaft. The mouth of that and the engine-house for the man-engine itself were on the area of rough ground just inland of the parking space. The stack there may be part of the original man-engine house, replaced in 1893 when a new horizontal engine was acquired. To quote from CAU: "For a site which should be a monument to one of the saddest disasters ever to strike a Cornish mine, this site is in a shamefully shabby condition." On the other side of the car park are the ruins of a little round explosives magazine, and there is another of these a few hundred yards along the track heading south-west.

Part of the huge area of dressing floors at Levant, photographed probably early this century. This was at the north-eastern end of the site, near what is now Geevor (towards the end of section 4 in the directions). The engine house in the distance on the left is the stamps, and the stack further right is that of the arsenic works The four small buildings with pointed roofs to the right of the stack housed the calciners. The buddles are of the type known as the round frame. A mixture of crushed ore and water was fed to the edges of the wooden saucer-like bowls, which revolved slowly. Since the heaviest particles are those containing cassiterite (tin stone, tin dioxide), as the "slime" gradually ran towards the centre the valuable material was deposited in the bowl while the "gangue" or tailings drained away at the centre. Brushes fixed to the superstructure helped with the separation process.

WALK 5
THE ST JUST MINES TRAIL
SECTION 5:
BOSCASWELL, PENDEEN
WATCH AND PORTHERAS
WITH A POSSIBLE EXTENSION TO
MORVAH

Just over 3 miles, or about 5 miles including Morvah

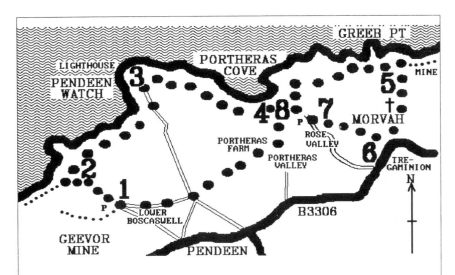

The mining remains may be less spectacular on this part of the "Trail" than on some of the earlier ones - certainly they are much less obvious, apart from the remains of Morvah Mine - but there is still plenty to interest the industrial archaeologist, and one section of the walk, the Portheras Valley, contains what CAU describes as "one of the most attractive and interesting groups of mining structures in West Cornwall." The coastal scenery is very fine, of course, and the lighthouse plus the church and tiny village of Morvah are other attractions. It is a moderately tough walk, with several steep and/or long climbs and - in winter at least - a good deal of glutinous mud, along with the possibility of rather overgrown paths here and there. If you want food and drink along the way you will need to take them with you, although cream teas are available near Portheras Cove in season according to a sign on the coast path.

The directions start at Lower Boscaswell. To drive there, take the coastward road heading north-west from the B3306 at Pendeen. If you are approaching from St Just, this is the first left turning after Pendeen church. After about half a mile you will come to a small "square" where there is room for a few cars to park. A good alternative would be Pendeen Watch, where there is a fair amount of parking space near the lighthouse. This can be reached by either of two minor roads from Pendeen. If you decide to start there, pick up the directions at point 3. A third possibility is the small car park at Lower Chypraze Farm above Portheras Cove. This is in the Rose Valley, at the seaward end of a minor road that leaves the B3306 just west of Morvah. For this, start following the directions just after the beginning of point 7.

1 From the "square", follow the sign "To Coast Path" - that is, continue in roughly the same direction as you have just driven or walked from Pendeen. After passing a small converted chapel or school and a few houses, fork left along a track between hedges, from which there is a good view to the left of the lower part of the Geevor Mine site (colour photo. 16). Where the track curves right into a field, turn left on to a narrow path which winds down, crossing a footbridge, to join the coast path.

2 Turn right on that. **Those doing the full St Just Mines Trail - start reading here.** There are far fewer mining remains on this section of coast than further south, but here and there you may see the odd small burrow. (One near the cliff edge may be a relic of Boscaswell Cliff Mine.) CAU also mentions leats and ponds hereabouts, but I did not notice them. When I walked this on a rather hazy day early in January 1993 the experience was rather dominated by deep booms issuing from a foghorn every 20 seconds or so, echoing eerily among the cliffs. The steepish climb up to Carn Ross, where there is a wooden stile, revealed the source of that sound: the lighthouse at Pendeen Watch, of which there is a fine view from here. The small stack a short way inland is part of an arsenic works at Trease, a relic of a short-lived attempt to reopen Boscaswell United Mine in 1907. Soon you reach the valley leading down to Mill Zawn, where there are two small streams to cross, and as the path goes up on the far side it takes you beside what looks like evidence of mining: old walls beside the stream, which seems to have been diverted across a flat area, plus a pond and perhaps the remains of dumps. Tin streaming was undoubtedly once carried on in this valley, but the visible relics are of a series of small water-powered dressing floors, most of them probably dating from the 1870s, used by various mines including Pendeen Consols, Boscaswell Cliff and Boscaswell Downs. Such tin-processing works were often known as mills, and the name of the zawn may derive from that, although it is equally likely that there was a corn mill in the valley. The coast path curves left and joins a road in front of a line of coastguards' cottages with a watchtower at the far end. As you approach the lighthouse the view eastwards opens up as far as Carn Galver and Gurnard's Head. Pendeen Lighthouse dates from 1900 and has a range of 28 miles. It is one of the last manned lighthouses remaining in Cornwall.

3 Heading east now on the coast path, you soon reach a gate, on the right-hand side of which is a fenced shaft, with what appear to be ruined mine buildings above. These are remains of Pendeen Consols, which had at least one pumping-engine house at or very near this site between 1853 and 1872. Before the lighthouse was built, the Pendeen Watch headland must have been dominated by mine buildings; if anything at all of them is left now, most of it is buried beneath the car park. The mine extended under the sea, where the richest deposits of tin, copper and lead were found to be. In its latter years Geevor extended its workings as far as this, and we were told that a very fine underground road gave access to the old Pendeen sett, "just like a motorway". Cross the stile on the left of the gate - notice the small burrow on the left - and soon you are approaching Portheras Cove. A tempting track down on the left leads past fishermen's sheds - the remains of pilchard cellars, according to Alfred J. Kliskey's little book, *A Walk through West Penwith, by a local coastguard* - to steep slipways and a rocky beach known as Boat Cove. "Besides a seine fishing station, this was the cove where the Pendeen miners have always kept their boats." (Dicon Nance: Trevithick Society Newsletter No. 22.) From there you can regain the coast path by a steep, narrow path. Edith Nicholas in StJP writes of the St Peter's Day (29 June) celebrations which used to take place on the clifftop here - there were various stalls, and a service accompanied by the Pendeen Silver Band. The tradition died out by 1951, but an attempt to revive it had been made in the '60s. Follow the coast path signs now. On an old gate is (or was) an advert for accommodation and cream teas available at the nearby Manor Farm, "as seen on BBC Poldark", but 11am on a January day didn't seem like the ideal time to go and sample what was on offer. (This is Pendeen Manor Farm, now a 500-acre dairy farm. The Manor Farm normally associated with "Poldark" is the one at Botallack - see Walk 3.)

4 Two streams rushing down steep little valleys meet just before flowing into the sea at Portheras Cove (colour photo. 17). If you want to do the full 5-mile walk you will now have to cross the combined waters - not an easy task in January after heavy rains, since there is no bridge. (If you prefer to limit yourself to the shorter walk, omitting Morvah, take the path up the first (Portheras) valley, picking up the directions at point 8.) To find the easiest crossing place, follow the main path almost down to beach level, then cut back sharply to where there are some makeshift stepping stones; a rough path goes up quite steeply from there on the far side. (If you decide to spend time on the beach first, do please heed the warnings about "Razor sharp fragments" resulting from attempts to remove the carcase of a wrecked ship.) Just after the sign warning about the danger to bathers there's a small cliff-edge path which leads to a good viewpoint, but from there you have either to return the same way or face a very steep, long climb up a rough path which in places near the top is somewhat overgrown with gorse. Better to keep to the official coast path, which curves right near the sign, goes up the valley for a few hundred yards and then is signposted sharp left. Once you're at the top of Carn Clough you'll have no trouble in following the coast path, which keeps well inland of Chypraze and Tregaminion Cliffs, thus making for half a mile-or-so of rather dull walking, despite the good view ahead. Perhaps there are more interesting side-paths nearer the sea. Not far beyond a wooden stile beside what looks like a small paddock the path curves still further inland, and stepping-stones plus a stile take you across a marshy area and a stream, with Morvah church and hamlet visible on the right. The little concrete-block shed near the stile contains what's left of Morvah Holy Well; beside it once

An unusual form of tin streaming, photographed - in very poor light, apparently - about 1925. Except for the fact that these pictures were taken at Portheras Cove, the description written by Lewis Hind fits closely: "In the cove by Cape Cornwall wire ropes are stretched from the beach to the summit of the cliff, and half a dozen men were loading buckets with sand, which were then whirled upwards on the ropes." (Days in Cornwall, *1907) He goes on to say that "this valuable sand, impregnated with tin" was washed in by the tides, and that the tin came from waste dumped in the sea at Botallack. A. K. Hamilton Jenkin visited the site here at Portheras in November 1926 - indeed, he may have taken the photos - and part of the note he made is worth quoting: "The venture is worked by two partners, and three men are employed. Six months' labour was required in bringing the water-wheels, pulveriser, timber for the sheds, etc., to this inaccessible place on the cliff. The actual place where the tin floors are erected was formerly the site of an old grist mill which was destroyed in the great flood of (?1890)*. There are remains of many stamps higher up the stream, where the ore from Rosemergy, the Garden Mine**, "Traze" (=Trease, part of Boscaswell) and other mines was treated. It is probably the tailings from these which is now being saved from the beach. It is collected by the men in hand barrows and with a cart drawn by two horses, and is brought up from thence on an "aerial", the bucket being drawn up the incline rope by a winch worked with a water-wheel." (Dr Jenkin also commented that these enterprising miners were an example to others, particularly to those who were "working to Wheal Easy",*

or drawing the dole in St Just.)   Work like this was still being carried on here and there well after World War II, whenever tin prices were high enough to make it pay.   An example mentioned to me by Mr Joff Bullen is one Wilfie Saar, who collected tin-bearing sand beneath the sheer cliffs at Cligga Head, near Perranporth, and took a lease on a small treatment works in Trevellas Coombe (the Jericho Valley) to process it.   The remains of the stamps still survive there: see Walk 5 in "A View from St Agnes Beacon".
* Probably November 1894: see Walk 8, point 4.
**On Watch Croft, where a ruined engine house can still be seen. Rosemergy was another name for Carn Galver Mine.

---

stood Tregaminion Chapel.

5 A few yards beyond the stream turn right.

You might, however, care to go about a quarter of a mile further along the coast path first to see the ruined engine house of Morvah Consols (*), which stands beside the path (colour photo. 19). It was built in 1874 for a 24" engine, used for both pumping and stamping - but it worked only for a year. A photograph of the building as it was in 1934 is in <u>CEH</u>, on page 6. The winding at this mine was done by a horse whim, which was sited north-east of the engine house in an area now fenced off. The ruined building on that side may be a remnant of the mine's smithy. Just west of the engine house is a walled yard containing substantial remains of dressing floors (colour photo. 20), including two convex buddles, now grassed over but easily recognisable. On the seaward side are many filled-in shafts and shallow pits, some of which seem to be being enlarged by badgers.

MORVAH CONSOLS

Although, in the words of <u>CAU</u>, "Morvah Mine probably never amounted to much," mining hereabouts has a long history: "Whele Chapel Morveth" was in existence nearly five centuries ago, probably as one of two streamworks in valleys east and west of the engine house; there was almost certainly some work done in the 18th century; the mine was active for several periods between about 1850 and 1880; and it was at least considered for re-opening in 1928. The only production figure recorded is 6 tons of black tin in 1873.

The inland path soon crosses the stream. Tin streaming used to take place here: see the reference to "Whele Chapel Morveth" in the note on Morvah Consols. A grassy path - muddy in places - brings you to Morvah (*) church. The tiny village flanking it is dominated by Merthyr farmhouse. The low building on the left of that was - so the farmer and his wife told me - a blacksmith's shop; the large circular stone propped against it used to lie flat, and was used in the process of making the iron bands that went round the rims of wooden wheels. Notice also the tiny Board School building dated 1882, with a very ancient petrol pump outside. The school closed in 1937; in its latter years it had one teacher and about 50 pupils.

MORVAH

Morvah parish is one of the smallest in Cornwall, at least in terms of population: according to a note in the church there were "53 people in the parish at the last count." The "churchtown" itself is tiny, but I was assured that 120 years ago, when the nearby mines were at their busiest, it was larger than Pendeen was then. Morvah Fair, held on the first Sunday in August, attracted large crowds in those days: a church document of 1850 refers to the "disorderly persons of every description" who assembled "for idle and profane amusement." Robert Hunt quotes a "Morva farmer" as saying, "A quarter of an acre would not hold the horses ridden to the fair, - the hedges being covered by the visitors, who drink and carouse as in former times. Morva Fair, however, is dying out." *(Popular Romances of the West of England,* 1881) Morvah's present sleepiness is quite recent: the little lane that winds through it was the main road till 1940. Its name is unusually interesting, even though the old belief that it derived from the Breton word "Morverch" ("Sea-daughters", mermaids) is now discounted. In fact it apparently means "sea grave", and the farm at its centre is called Merthyr, "place with a saint's relics". Together the names would seem to amount to "saint's grave by the sea", but who was the saint? Not "St Morwetha" or "St Morveth", both of which are inventions derived from the word Morvah; not St Bridget or Briget of Sweden, to whom the church is dedicated: she died in Rome. Oliver Padel suggests it may have been the "Sanctus Morianus martyr" who according to William of Worcester (1478) was buried above the seashore west of Penzance. (CPN) A church was built here in the 14th century, probably on the site of an ancient Chapel of St Briget; the dedication to her has prompted considerable interest on the part of Swedish people, who have made several gifts to the church. Of the medieval building only the tower remains; the rest was demolished and rebuilt in 1828.

6 Walk past Merthyr farmhouse (that is, turn right on leaving the church). One of the cottages you pass once contained a cobbler's shop. You now have a short stretch of the B3306 to walk along: please take great care, and walk facing the oncoming traffic, which can be quite heavy in summer. The house you soon reach bears the name Tregaminion Manor: "the chief place, and almost the only one of note in this little parish," wrote Thomas Tonkin (1736). From Tudor times it belonged to the Lanyon family, from whom perhaps Lanyon Quoit is named - but Lanyon means "cold pool" or "cold stream", and the family may have taken its name from the place. Opposite the post box there is a metal gate, with a not-very-obvious stile just past it. Cross that. Cows had churned the area just beyond into a morass when I was there, but in summer it should be better. Cross the field to a second stile, about 25 yards to the right of the corner, and continue in the same line to a third and fourth, the last of which is in a field corner opposite a house called Wheal Rose. (There is, however, no evidence of a mine of that name in these parts.)

7 Turn right on the minor road leading down to Rose Valley, which soon takes you past the car park at Lower Chypraze. The path from the farm crosses what looks like a leat and then runs for a while beside the stream. A little lower down, where the path is further from the stream, there are the

remains of quite substantial old cornmill buildings. Continue downhill to join the coast path above Portheras Cove, and cross the stream via the stepping stones, as before. (See point 4.)

8 When you reach the coast path post on the far side, go straight on - that is, up the Portheras Valley (*). (Colour photo. 18) The path is clear but narrow at first, with gorse and brambles threatening to grow over it; later it widens, and was extremely muddy in places in January owing to the visits of cows. Before you have gone many yards you will see the ruins of quite large buildings down by the stream, and many of them are fairly accessible by means of various little side paths. The Archaeological Unit's survey has identified at least eight stamping-mill sites in this short valley (often referred to as Oxman's Stamps) and unravelled the complexity of the system by which leats transferred water from the Rose Valley to this one. It is a wonderful place to explore, and you may enjoy trying to draw your own conclusions before reading what Adam Sharpe has to say.

9 Just beyond two substantial ruins on the far side of the stream, there is a small stone bridge. Don't cross that, but take the muddy uphill path on your right, which curves sharp right and left. Cross the stile beside a metal gate and go on up to the farm buildings (Portheras Farm) via a path between hedges. Turn left at the farm; ignore the stile on the left, but cross the one on the right a few yards later, then walk beside the wall on your left. (The view to your left now includes the prominent pair of engine houses of Wheal Hearle or East Boscaswell - working period 1853-75 - which stand beside the B3318 road from Pendeen to Penzance; and further right is the tower of Pendeen's 19th-century church.) Cross a stile on your left and another on your right just after that, so that now the hedge is on your right. Another stile and a boggy patch bring you to Calartha Farm, where a pair of dogs created plenty of sound and fury that day, signifying nothing much. One more stile and a path between hedges leads to a farm lane. Fork right, and then go straight on into Lower Boscaswell at the crossroads. To return to the suggested parking place keep right in the village, where the traditional miners' cottages are conveniently set opposite modern efforts for comparison. Considering the very high level of unemployment in this area, especially since Geevor closed, I was surprised how few "For Sale" signs there were. **At the 'square', if you are doing the full St Just Mines Trail keep straight on along a track leading into the Geevor site, as described in Walk 4, starting at line 3 of point 6.**

THE PORTHERAS VALLEY

Some mining may have taken place in the valley (see the note on St Just United, Walk 2), but its main historical interest results from the fact that nearby mines brought their tin here to be dressed. There were also corn mills, but most of them were in the Rose Valley. To satisfy the needs of all the stamping mills, supplementary supplies of water had to be taken from the Rose stream, by means of leats which ran at a high level around Chyrose Cliff (the seaward end of the steep hill that divides the two streams: colour photo 17). Adam Sharpe argues that the need for this water to be returned to the corn mills in the lower part of the Rose Valley explains why so many of the stamping mills in the Portheras Valley had to be built on cramped sites at the upper end. The Archaeological Unit's survey found remains of eleven water-powered sites in the two valleys: three corn mills and eight stamps. Ten of them appear to have been in use - or at any rate their buildings were still in reasonable condition - during the 1870s, but of those all but two were derelict by 1908. The eleventh was a small set of stamps erected in the mid-1920s near the mouth of the valley: see page 72. How long that operated seems not to be on record. The CAU's analysis of the management of water power in these two valleys is, I think, among the most impressive things in its St Just publication, and it has convinced me of the truth of Mr Sharpe's comment: "Almost all the buildings in these water-powered sites are in desperate need of conservation if they are not, within a few more decades, to disappear completely from the West Penwith landscape. That loss, were it to happen, would be tragic."

WALK 6
CARN GALVER, PORTHMEOR, BOSIGRAN CASTLE AND PORTHMOINA

About 4 miles, including the walk up Carn Galver (about 1.5 miles), which can be omitted or done separately.

You should include the Carn Galver part of this route ONLY in reasonably clear conditions, because it would be easy to get lost among the narrow, winding paths if you can't see far ahead.

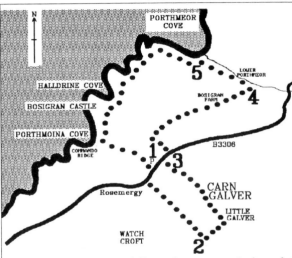

Scenically this is a very fine walk: breathtaking cliffs cut by deep coves and zawns; two attractive short valleys; bare moorland littered with granite boulders, rising to one of the best-known and most beautiful tors in Penwith, from which in clear weather the view stretches from Zennor to the heart of the St Just mining district as well as inland to Ding Dong Mine - hence my choice of title. *Even though the mines in this area were very insignificant compared with those near St Just, the principal mining remains hereabouts are exceptionally well preserved and accessible, thanks to the work of the National Trust. There is plenty of evidence of very early habitation, especially around the Carn, on Bosigran cliff and at Porthmeor. Of modern habitation, however, there is precious little - just three farms on or near the route - so once again you will have to take with you any provisions you may need. Good stout footwear is essential, especially on and around Carn Galver, but also on parts of the coast path, and the field paths around Bosigran Farm tend to be very muddy. The climb to the ridge of the Carn is fairly tough unless you are used to hill walking, and there is a steep ascent from Porthmeor Cove. The National Trust's "Coast of Cornwall" leaflet No. 10 is a very useful companion on this walk, especially in connection with the engine houses and the Porthmoina Tin Stamps. Its author, Des Hannigan, has also described a variation of the walk detailed here in* **WW** - *particularly useful if you want information on the natural history and geology of the area. Much of this route, extended to include Gurnard's Head, is described briefly but entertainingly by Gerald Priestland in* **WHR***; he writes particularly vividly about the rock types and formations.*

The directions are given from the small National Trust car park beside the engine houses of Carn Galver Mine, on the B3306 just east of Rosemergy.

1 Perhaps it's best to start with the Carn, while you've still got plenty of energy! This part of the walk shouldn't take much more than an hour, or 90 minutes at the most, at the end of which you could return to your car for refreshments. If you would prefer to do the coastal walk first, however, set off along the road in the St Ives direction and start reading at the second sentence in point 3. For the hill walk, go 100 yards-or-so along the road in the St Just direction towards the sizeable group of farm buildings, Rosemergy. Turn left at the public footpath sign. The path is pretty rough and in places soggy; in places it seems to double as the bed of a stream. Keep to the most obvious path, heading to the right of the hilltop, Carn Galver (*).

CARN GALVER

The name, sometimes written as Carn or Cairn Galva, means "rock-pile of the look-out place": compare the nearby, slightly higher hill, Watch Croft. (An alternative explanation of the name, "Goats' Carn", is not mentioned by Padel. Compare "Geevor".) The highest point on the Carn Galver ridge (at the inland end) is 816 feet above sea level. A stone enclosure, probably as much as 5,000 years old, was identified on the slopes of Carn Galver by the Cornwall Archaeological Unit in 1984; it may have acted as a defensive wall for a group of wooden huts. In Cornish legend Cairn Galva is the home of the Giant Holiburn, "a very amiable and somewhat sociable gentleman," according to Robert Hunt's *Popular Romances of the West of England* (1881). He ran a sort of protection racket, guarding the local human beings from the aggressive Trencrom giants in return for gifts of sheep and cattle. He married a farmer's daughter and begat "a very fine race", but his love of boisterous games with "human pigmies" led to an unfortunate incident when a playful tap on the head of a peasant "scattered his brains on the grass."

---

2 After about half a mile the path levels off and a low stone wall begins on the left; fork left there, and then take the side path starting at a gap in the wall, heading for the ridge now. There is, in fact, quite a number of fairly indistinct paths to choose among. I recommend that you aim for the highest outcrop, at the right-hand end of the ridge (rather oddly known as Little Galver), where it's worth scrambling up to the top for the excellent view south-east, dominated by the lonely engine house of Ding Dong mine (visited on Walk 7), with St Michael's Mount beyond, and the Lizard and Tregoning and Godolphin Hills in the far distance. You may be able to make out the engine house of Great Work mine on the left-hand slope of Tregoning. (Something we missed at the top of Carn Galver, probably because we were concentrating on the view, is a half-finished millstone. It's worth looking for, because the method used for splitting the granite, by making use of the fact that wood swells when it is wet, suggests that it was made before 1800.) To continue the walk along the ridge towards the coast involves a lot of scrambling - sometimes over the top, more often just to left or right of it - but is very worthwhile for the beautiful rock shapes on the Carn itself and the ever-developing view of the coastal strip, said by geologists to have been covered by the sea in very ancient times, and the nearby hills such as Watch Croft to the left and Hannibal's Carn and Zennor Hill to the right, which must have formed the headlands then. From the seaward end of the ridge you should be able to make out the church towers of Zennor, Pendeen and Morvah (the last quite close); Pendeen Lighthouse is prominent, and visible engine houses or stacks include those at Levant. The closest clifftop features are Commando Ridge and Bosigran Castle on either side of Porthmoina Cove; further right are Porthmeor Cove, Carn Gloose and a glimpse of Gurnard's Head. Now your task is to follow the rather rambling and in places indistinct path among huge granite boulders down to the twin engine houses and former count house of Carn Galver Mine (*). If you manage to keep to the "official" path you should reach the road opposite the count house, now adopted by the Climbers' Club of Great Britain, whose members find Commando Ridge and the Bosigran Main Face a particularly exciting challenge. "The wrinkled sea beneath them crawls," writes Gerald Priestland,

Carn Galver Mine: the pumping-engine house

79

CARN GALVER MINE

As is so often the way with particularly impressive or prominent engine houses, these are relics of a comparatively unsuccessful mine. (Other examples are Wheal Coates near St Agnes, Trevoole near Praze-an-Beeble, Nancegollan near Helston, Pennance on the slopes of Carn Marth, Ventonwyn overlooking the A38 west of St Austell - and, within the area covered by this book, the Higher Bal section of Levant. One could provide a list at least as long of great mines which have left little evidence on the surface that they ever existed: St Ives Consols and Providence Mine above Carbis Bay would be among them.) Carn Galver, alias Wheal Rose or Rosemergy, is recorded as having produced 150 tons of tin in the 1860s and '70s, when it was part of a group called Morvah and Zennor United - a separate company from Morvah Consols, by the way. Both engine houses were built in 1871, so they had a short active life: the mine had closed by 1876. (December 1871, given as the closure date in NT10, should read December 1873, which is when the company went into liquidation. It would seem that some work continued after that, because Dines refers to output figures for 1871-6.) Nearly forty years earlier, the mine appears to have been more prosperous than in its last re-working, since Collins says that in 1838 it "had a 40-inch engine and employed 116 people" (WEMR); A. K. Hamilton Jenkin, however, assumes that these figures refer to Morvah and Zennor Mines rather than Carn Galver alone. Carn Galver Mine's workings were drained by an adit about half a mile long leading into the engine shaft, now filled, which lies adjacent to the half-fallen engine house. The adit's mouth can be seen at the back of Porthmoina Cove. Dr Jenkin gives interesting details about how this adit was driven, between 1851 and 1869, and how the considerable problems of ventilation in it were solved. For a much fuller account of that and the general history of the mine, see CNSI. Noall tells how a disaster similar to the later one at Wheal Owles (Walk 3) was averted as the new adit drew close to old workings containing "a vast body of water, say about 400 feet deep and near 1,000 feet long" (*Cornish Telegraph* 10.4.1867). An iron bar was driven some 4-6 feet ahead of the main excavation, and when this broke through to the "house of water" the miners had time to escape while the underground lake drained gently into the sea.

adapting Tennyson; "and every now and then, one falls." Vivid photographs of climbers on these cliffs are included in yet another of Des Hannigan's publications, *Bosigran and the North Coast* (Climbers' Club Guides to West Penwith, 1991). The count house has associations with the poet and novelist D. H. Lawrence. Some details about his period of residence near Zennor during World War I are given in Walk 8. At that time the count house was let to the composer Philip Heseltine, better known as Peter Warlock. Lawrence and his German wife Frieda would occasionally visit for evening meals, and one night when they were there a flapping curtain at a lit window was interpreted by local patriots as signals to enemy submarines. However ludicrous this may seem now, it led directly to the Lawrences' being ordered to leave Cornwall late in 1917.

3 At the road turn right, unless you want to return to your car first. The small ruined building on the right was the mine's gunpowder house and smithy. (So says NT10, but if it was both at once I'm not surprised it's in ruins!) Just before the road bends, take the wide track on the left, then cross the stile beside a metal gate and turn right. You have a rather boggy patch to cross at first, and there is no obvious path. (The NT leaflet describes this as "Church Path". Evidently churchgoers don't make much use of the path nowadays. The path is still sometimes called "Church road": an ancient packhorse road, it formed the link between all the settlements from St Ives to St Just until the existing road was built in the 17th century.) The right of way heads north-east for Bosigran Farm in a fairly straight line, keeping quite close to the hedge on the right most of the way. At the first field boundary there is a small gate for walkers beside the farm gate; at the second, a very rough stile in the hedge to the left of the gap; then the path curves a little to the right, and you pass through two more gaps before reaching the approach to the farm buildings - an extremely muddy area in January. At the farmyard go slightly left and cross the impressive stone stile accompanied by a NT footpath sign - rather less helpful here than it could have been at several points earlier. The path runs fairly straight ahead, through a few gaps - there's another footpath sign. Don't make for the sea yet, but continue down into the Porthmeor ("great cove") Valley, over two more big stiles, heading a little inland of a small chimney. A spring just before the first stile creates boggy conditions at most times of year, but beyond the stile the water is channelled into what looks like a leat - perhaps to provide a water supply to the tinworks in the valley, although obviously the main Porthmeor stream was its principal power source.

4 Turn left immediately beyond the second stile, following the signpost to the coast path. The tin treatment plant is an excellent example, and perhaps the best place of any visited on walks in this book to illustrate the various processes. Des Hannigan's leaflet (NT10) states that it was used by Carn Galver Mine from about 1850, when the mine's needs outgrew the nearer tin-dressing complex at Porthmoina; according to Barry Atkinson (MSC) it was used by Morvah Consols, a different enterprise: see Walk 5. Dressing floors like this may well have been run by independent companies who competed for business, like the smelting houses. The pit for the waterwheel that worked the stamps is near the top of the site; an old, rusty sluice gate can still be seen in the main leat that runs through the works; below are buddles and an old-style calciner with small stack still intact. (Colour photo. 21) This calciner appears to be similar in design to the one in the Cot Valley mentioned in Walk 1 (point 3), and may be of the same date: an article in *The Cornishman* of 29th November 1901 refers to "the tin stamps being erected at Portmeor, Zennor". OS maps show that there were tin processing works here by 1877, however. Just below the stack, on the left side of the path, is a rather mysterious little stone chamber, like a miniature fogou; Des Hannigan in WW calls it a "field shelter ... which may be a relic of early settlement." Such little shelters, like the fishermen's huts at Priest's Cove (Walk 2), are called "crows" in the St Just area. Further down the valley is a group of rectangular settling tanks. At least one corn or grist mill was powered by the Porthmeor stream, but which if any of the visible ruins are a relic of that I don't know. Since it was in use "pre-1800" according to NT10, all trace may well have gone now.

5 As you reach the rather boggy area on the cliffs above the cove you may need to hunt around a little to pick up the coast path heading west (left). There is, in fact, another small NT sign. The path runs about 15 yards inland from the·cliff-edge fence and then crosses it by means of a wooden stile. There follows a very rough section, easy to stumble on, as you climb "bald tor", Carn Moyle. Please don't stumble where the path runs disconcertingly close to a deep zawn, made the more fearsome by the blackness of the rock here. The next hilltop, and also the headland below it, give a fine view from Gurnard's Head to Pendeen lighthouse. Another zawn follows, and there's a stile to cross before you reach Halldrine Cove (the name possibly means "moor of thorn-bushes"). A fairly stiff climb takes you to Bosigran Castle (*), from which there is a fine view of Porthmoina Cove, with its small waterfall. ("Porthmoina" sounds as if it ought to mean "little cove", in contrast to Porthmeor, but "moina" probably derives from a personal name. J. T. Blight in *A Week at the Land's End* states that it means Monk's Cove, but explanations of Cornish place-names in 1876 were very unreliable.) Beyond the cove is Commando Ridge, so called because it was used to train Marine Commandos during and for a few years after World War II. The stream that creates the waterfall runs in a deep little canyon beside the fascinating remains of the Porthmoina Tin Stamps (colour photo. 22). Rosemary Robertson's reconstruction of this site (reproduced in NT10) is very helpful; in case you do not have it with you, I'll explain a few of the more important features. What looks like a gable end is in fact part of the wheelpit. Water was taken from the stream higher up the valley and conducted by a leat and launder to a large overshot waterwheel which drove the Cornish stamps machine, housed in a shed the roofline of which is clear. (The tinners seem to have adapted an existing cornmill to their needs, and the gable end indicates the size of the original building.) The water from the wheel was then led to a series of rectangular buddles and settling tanks in which the stamped ore was washed. CNSI (page 107) includes details of the enlargement of "Bossigran Stamps" in 1860-1: a 36-foot waterwheel with a new set of twelve heads of stamps plus two new patent Borlase's round buddles, 20 feet in diameter, were installed. Unlike the Porthmeor plant, this one does not seem to have had a calciner for burning off impurities such as arsenic before the tin was taken for smelting. Incidentally, my wife and I caused much annoyance, as we wandered around the tinworks site, to a small flock of spectacular sheep grazing there, among which was a fearsome-looking ram with a pair of long straight horns in addition to the little curly ones sported by the ewes. We later learnt, from a rather battered NT notice, that these animals are a rare breed from the Isle of Man called Loughtons. As you follow the path up the valley you may notice the remains of several ponds (reservoirs to enable the tinworks to keep going in times of drought) and ruined structures which are evidence of older stamping mills. The various small hummocks and pits may be relics of early tin streaming and openwork mining. The largest pond, still full of water, is a little further west and not visible from this path - you will probably have noticed it from Carn Galver; the water in that one was used for the steam engines in the two restored (or, perhaps more accurately, consolidated) engine houses. (The last colour photograph shows the scene as you approach them.) The photograph on pages 12-13 of the NT leaflet (also in MMC, CNSI and several other publications) is excellent if you want to understand the various structures beside the car park. The tall stack was part of the pumping engine house, where a 30" beam engine drew water from a 780-feet-deep shaft on the seaward side; the more complete building was for the 20" winding engine which drew "back to front" from the same shaft, and the wheelpit built for the drum of the whim is still in good order. There was a separate chimney, the base of which is not far from the shaft; perhaps this stack was for the whim engine, but the NT leaflet states it was earlier in date than these engine houses.

BOSIGRAN CASTLE

The name probably means "dwelling-house of the crane" - the bird, that is; as Des Hannigan mentions in NT10, the romantic notion that this was the site of the home of Ygrain, King Arthur's mother, has no basis in known fact. Mr Hannigan proposes "dwelling place in the dry valley" as an alternative explanation of "Bosigran", referring to the farm from which the headland is named. There is, of course, no "castle" here in the sense usually associated with the Knights of the Round Table: the promontory was a fortified settlement in Iron Age times, some 2,000 years ago. There seems to have been just one rampart across the wide neck of the headland. No trace has been found of dwellings within the "castle", but quite substantial remains of several courtyard houses from that period are nearby, and the headland may have been fortified as a possible refuge in case of emergency. The pattern of fields worked by Iron Age farmers still survives on this part of the coastal strip.

WALK 7
MADRON & DING DONG MINE

A little over 6 miles

This inland walk is magnificent in very clear weather, when the panoramic views are unforgettable. The mine buildings are almost as impressive as their setting amidst the bare upland moors of Penwith, surrounded by evidence of prehistoric man and ringed by the far horizon; and to the industrial archaeologist they are of great interest both historically and technically. The walk is based on the old village of Madron, which has a fine medieval church - a treasurehouse of beautiful and/or historically interesting objects - and many other attractive buildings. A short diversion enables you to visit an ancient ruined chapel and nearby holy well. I must admit that I took the holy well on trust, because several days of teeming rain immediately before I did this walk had made it inaccessible to anyone not kitted out with wellies. The same applied to one of the field paths I had planned to use on the return half of the route; luckily there were quiet little country roads as an alternative, and the mud in no way spoilt the walk for me. Nevertheless, if you particularly dislike road walking - and one should bear in mind that some of the roads are likely to be less quiet in July and August than they were for me in January - you may well wish to try the path for yourself, so I will indicate it on my sketch map, and if you also arm yourself with the Pathfinder map you will probably get through perfectly satisfactorily, because the paths and stiles in Madron parish seem to be pretty well maintained. Madron has a shop and a pub, but for the rest of the walk you are out in the wilds.

MADRON

The name of the village is said to be derived from that of a Celtic saint called Maddern, about whom nothing is known, not even his or her gender. Charles Henderson stated in his notes written before 1924 that the word "Madron" is pronounced "Maddern", but it is rarely if ever heard in that form nowadays. (Joan Tregenza, the heroine of *Lying Prophets,* uses the old pronunciation.) A farm near the church was called Landithy, and this has led to speculation that an earlier saint called Dithy may have founded the first church here, but there seems to be little support from modern scholars for this theory. Landithy is mentioned by Henry Jennings (Vicar from 1922 to 1941) in MMP as the residence of the Knights of St John - presumably a lodging-house for pilgrims to the Holy Land. A Charter of King John in 1206 declared "the Church of St Madern de Runeri" (Runeri probably refers to Roseworthy in Gwinear) to be the property of the Knights of St John. Canon Jennings gives an interesting account of the origins and history of that body and its connection with the St John Ambulance Brigade. Until 1867 Madron parish was one of the largest in the county, including the whole of Penzance and part of Newlyn, and it was only as recently as 1985 that Morvah parish was separated from Madron. The church, like so many others in Cornwall, contains a few traces of a Norman building but is mostly from the 14th and 15th centuries, and was very heavily restored by J. P. St Aubyn in 1887 as well as by others since then. It is very spacious and has an exceptionally fine collection of monuments including the impressive slate memorial to the son of the first Mayor of Penzance, John Maddern (died 1621) - whose surname, I presume, was derived from his family's parish. An inscribed stone, probably of the 6th or 7th century, discovered in 1936 under nine layers of plaster, is now clearly visible beneath a stained-glass window in the south west corner. Another object of special note is a panel of ten angels carved in alabaster, probably from the 14th century; this is on the south wall of the Lady Chapel. Notice also the medieval bench-ends in the Chapel, and the carved roof bosses. Among the best-known exhibits in the church is the Nelson Banner, which was made in 1805 to celebrate the victory at Trafalgar as well as to mourn the Admiral's death: Penzance fishermen had been the first to report the news in England. The banner is in a glass case near the north door. On all sides there are well-labelled relics and photographs of the church before restoration, and the excellent guidebook available in the church lists and describes most of them. Of special interest (I trust!) to readers of this book is the "Ding Dong Bell", which like the banner and the Maddern tablet is near the north door. A notice states that it was "last rung in 1878 to bring up the final shift of miners". In a display case are "tin marks" used in the parish since the 12th century. Canon Jennings' history of the parish has a particularly detailed and fascinating chapter on the administration of the poor law in Madron. It was at Madron Workhouse (the remains of which can still be seen, as mentioned in the directions) that the St Ives rag-and-bone merchant and "primitive" artist Alfred Wallis died in 1942, despite the celebrity his work had already begun to achieve through the patronage of Ben Nicholson, Barbara Hepworth and others. They paid for his funeral, though, and he is buried at Barnoon cemetery in St Ives.

There is a small public car park beside the lych-gate of Madron (*) church. To drive to that, turn left as you enter the village, coming from the Penzance/Heamoor direction. Notice beside the church the village school, the subject of an excellent publication by the local WI in 1978. It was founded early in the 18th century by George Daniel, the son of Alexander Daniel, whose tomb bears an epitaph that's quoted in all the guide books. Just to be different, I'll leave you to find it for yourself. It's in the graveyard, near the south door of the church.

1 From the main entrance to the church, on the north side, walk along the road straight ahead, passing the Thomas Simon Bolitho Institute and Landithy Hall (which looks like a group of almshouses but is described in the church guide as the village hall) on your left, and the William IV ("Circa 1700") on your right at the corner. There turn left along Fore Street, past the post office/stores - the odd-shaped building opposite, now a garage, was the blacksmith's shop - and continue for about a quarter of a mile, passing the Madron Methodist Church and the overflow graveyard. A small group of old cottages on the right bear the name Mount View, and this is an accurate promise of what is to come on the walk, provided you have heeded my advice to choose a clear day. *A very short diversion to the end of the road on the right, also called Mount View, will bring you to the abbatoir, the Madron Meat Co., which occupies the remains of the old Madron Workhouse - the "gaunt" building whose "ashy walls" Jane Tregenza passed on her way to*

Madron Well. "She shivered as she passed, and was sad, knowing that a whole world of poverty, failure, sorrow, regret, lay hidden in that cold, still pile." (Eden Phillpotts: *Lying Prophets,* 1897) *Return the same way to the main road.*

2 Cross the stile beside the last house on the right and walk with the hedge on your right. After two stiles the path runs between hedges and comes to a minor road. Already you have a view ahead of two of the three surviving engine houses of Ding Dong; the tall hill furthest to the right is Castle-an-Dinas, recognisable by the large quarry near the top and the folly known as Rogers' Tower above it. (See Walk 1 in *A View from Trencrom.)*

3 Turn right on the road.

For the short diversion to Madron Baptistry and Wishing Well (*),.turn right again immediately on to a track, and then take the path on the left after a few yards. The path was muddy in January, and in fact just beyond a stile it doubled as a small stream for a short distance. Hundreds of assorted rags tied to low branches plus a sign pointing left indicated the proximity of the Well, but as I said in the introductory note I decided against trying to paddle

MADRON BAPTISTRY AND WELL

The site of the tiny chapel may have been the spot chosen by St Maddern for his oratory - and perhaps before him by St Dithy. The ruins there now are, of course, much later in date, although the lower parts are claimed to be pre-Norman. The "font" inside it, and also the "wishing well" about a hundred yards away, have always been credited with great powers of healing. The miraculous cure of the crippled John Trelille in about 1640 was told in detail by Bishop Hall of Exeter a few years later, and there are many accounts of mothers bathing their children in the water and performing other rituals. The separate well may once have been enclosed in a well-house, and Charles Henderson in <u>CHN</u> states that there were formerly steps leading down to the well, but there is no sign of any of that now, and indeed many changes have been made to chapel, well and stream over the centuries. For example, the well-water was, according to the church guidebook, "the main supply to Penzance up to 1830", and much more recently it was still being "piped down to Madron as a domestic water supply." (P. O. & D. V. Leggatt: *The Healing Wells)* The leat carrying it ran beside the parish church until the churchyard was extended during the 1820s. The custom that pilgrims should tie a piece of cloth to a twig near the well as proof of their visit or as an offering to the saint is very ancient; according to Quiller Couch it is done in many countries to protect cattle, propitiate the fairies or stave off the sorcery of the Druids. This mixture of Christian and pagan belief is well captured by Joan Tregenza in the Eden Phillpotts novel. (See part 1 of the directions.) Speaking of the rags "tored off a petticoat, or some sich thing" by mothers after dipping their babies naked in the brook, she says, "They hanged 'em up around about on the thorn bushes, to shaw as they'd 'a' done more for the good saint if they'd had the power. An' theer's another marvellous thing as washin' in thicky waters done: it kep' the fairies off - the bad fairies I mean, 'cause there'm good an' bad piskies, same as good an' bad men folks."

through to it. The way ahead to the Baptistry was clear, however, and it proved to be a delightful spot: a beautiful little ruined chapel, complete with altar (colour photo. 23) and a font supplied with flowing water. Nearby is an explanatory notice, sadly vandalised and only partially legible. To continue the walk, return the same way and turn right on reaching the road.

Before long there is an old and very worn Celtic cross beside the road. Where the road bears right to Boswarthen Farm, continue ahead on the surfaced path, forking left up to a stile splashed with orange paint. From there go straight on across the field (but pause a moment and look back at the superb view of Mount's Bay, with the Goonhilly Satellite Earth Station dishes visible on the skyline way beyond the Mount) to a stile on the left of a gateway. The path continues straight ahead, crossing four more stiles, the last of which brings you to the main Madron - Morvah road.

4 Fork right immediately on to a minor road. As this gradually climbs towards Ding Dong it gives you a view to the left of Lanyon Quoit (though you may have trouble finding it, since it is half a mile away and below the skyline), and almost behind you, with the sea horizon beyond it, can be seen the tall tower of St Buryan church. After passing the entrance to Bosiliack Farm the road dwindles to a rough track, which soon brings you to the beautiful Greenburrow Shaft engine house of Ding Dong Mine (*). From that the view is even more panoramic - one of the finest in Cornwall, in fact - and includes the rocky tor of Carn Galver (see Walk 6), the rounder Watch Croft on its left, and the ancient settlement of Chûn Castle further left again.

Well within a mile of this spot are the famous ancient monuments known as the Mên an Tol (holed stone), the Mên Scryfa (inscribed stone) and the Nine Maidens (the Boskednan stone circle), and the OS maps indicate what looks like a simple little circular route on paths that would include all three. I don't advise you to try it, however, unless you are equipped with wellies, gorse-proof trousers, a compass, a large-scale map and advanced orienteering skills. No doubt I am exaggerating the problem, but perhaps that's understandable after I had wasted an hour trying to decide among several dozen equally likely-looking little paths, all of which ended in bogs or impenetrable gorse or both! There are several other books or leaflets suggesting walks that visit these sites, so if you're keen to see them I'll leave you in their capable hands.

Let's take a look at the engine house and its immediate surroundings now. (For many of the details that follow I am much indebted to Kenneth Brown and Gerald Williams, who led a field trip at Ding Dong Mine for the Trevithick Society in September 1989.) This best-known of the three recognisable engine houses on the site (colour photo. 27) was built in 1865 for a 40" engine which pumped from the 480-feet-deep shaft it stands beside as well as from Ding Dong Shaft, several hundred yards to the north-east, by means of flat-rods. (The engine used at Greenburrow had worked at Ding Dong Shaft until 1865.) Twice this century the dumps of mine waste around the building have been sifted for the residues of metals they contain; quite recently Geevor Mine applied to work them over again, but local environmentalists objected and permission was denied. The engine house

DING DONG MINE

This is reputedly one of the oldest mines in Cornwall. Dines (MMR) mentions the claim that some of its lodes were discovered "in distant, possibly in pre-historic, times," and the legend that Jesus Christ visited Cornwall sometimes includes Ding Dong Mine on the itinerary. To Cornish engineers, Ding Dong is best known for the 28"-cylinder inverted engine designed by Edward ("Ned") Bull, which was put up at Ding Dong Shaft in 1796, and which infringed James Watt's Patent. Watt sent his lawyers who nailed an injunction on the engine-house door, following which Richard Trevithick altered Bull's engine to exhaust to atmosphere. This was one of several attempts to infringe Watt's condenser patent prior to 1800 of which there is record. (Another example, at Wheal Unity near St Day, is described in *The Landfall Book of the Poldice Valley,* on page 65.) The mine's main active period began in 1814. By 1850 it was employing about a hundred people. The most conspicuous engine house, on Greenburrow Shaft, was built in 1865 for a 40" pumping engine which was transferred from the old engine shaft in the centre of the sett. By 1874 the mine had five beam engines and a work force of 273, but there was little tin ore left, and when prices fell to £41 per ton in 1877 the decision was taken to close. During the following months an effort was made to re-open it, but the re-constituted company was finally dissolved in 1880. Unsuccessful attempts to re-work the mine were made in 1912 and 1928. Its name, which took the form of "Dindods" in the 13th century according to MMP, has led to a good deal of speculation. As well as another Ding Dong mine near Gunnislake on the Devon-Cornwall border there were Bal Ding in Wendron parish, Wheal Ding near Lanivet and Ting Tang Mine near St Day. Canon Jennings mentions the suggestion that "Ding Dong" means "head of the lode", referring to an outcrop of tin on the hill. The "Ding Dong bell" displayed in Madron church is, of course, much more modern than the name.

was consolidated in the late 1980s under the Manpower Services scheme.

5 *Before continuing the main walk, you might care to cross the rough stile beside the gate near the engine house and go a little way along the track that runs westwards from there, with the "Hooting Carn" (Carn Kenidjack, above St Just) ahead in the distance. This diversion provides a good view of several deep pits, open shafts, and so on, left by the miners. A good many shafts at Ding Dong lurk unsuspected and unprotected among the gorse and bracken, so it is important not to wander off the recognised paths. (Further over to the left is a well preserved and impressive ancient monument, the Bosiliack Chambered Cairn; unfortunately it is on private ground and not visible from the footpath.) Take the same way back to the engine house.*
Return to the main track by which you came up from Madron and turn left on it. It curves right and heads north-east through an area where reminders of the mine are visible almost everywhere. On the left are several fenced shafts, and half-hidden by the scrub covering the rough ground on the right are old walls surviving from the dressing floors, among them the foundations of a stamps engine house (24"-cylinder engine) and part of the embankment which

carried a tramway from the Tredinnick Shaft at the eastern end of the mine to the battery of 40 or possibly 44 stamps. Where the track curves right, a metal farm gate on the right marks the entrance to the site of a whim-engine house, now gone. Not far beyond that is the 480-feet-deep Ding Dong Shaft, the one which was linked by flat-rods to the Greenburrow engine. Quite close to the small group of houses are two shafts: Hard Shaft on the right of the track and Ishmael's on the left. In 1868 the mine decided to drain Ishmael's, which had been flooded below the 70-foot level for at least 20 years. Two men who went down to fit siphons were badly scalded in an explosion, and soon afterwards the mine manager and four other miners had similar experiences. When Davy lamps were taken down the shaft it was found that the problem resulted from fire damp (methane gas) caused by the timbers which had lain rotting for so long. Though a well-known hazard in coal mines, fire damp was one of the few dangers not normally faced by Cornish miners. The engine house held a whim engine, probably 25"; the masonry wall beside it shows where the whim drum was mounted, and the fact that it lines up with the Tredinnick (or Tredinneck - the name means "gorse farm") Shaft, beside the third engine house, indicates that it hauled from that one. Go on down the road now to visit the Tredinnick engine house, whose engine, a short-stroke 30", pumped not only from Tredinnick Shaft - the deepest in the mine at 135 fathoms - but also from Providence Shaft (110 fathoms) about 150 yards to the west, by means of flat-rods. The engine house, built about 1830, is said to have used some granite taken from the "Nine Maidens" stone circle, which despite its name probably originally had nineteen stones, eight of which are no longer *in situ.* Kenneth Brown tells me that one such stone is clearly visible in the west wall of the engine house. To continue the walk, carry on down the road past several houses.

6 Turn right along the short lane which starts just before a house named Chynoweth - there is a wooden garage on the right at the start of the lane - and cross the big stone stile on your left almost at the end of the lane. Now walk with the hedge on your left, cross a second stile beside an open gateway and continue in the same direction through a second gap but don't follow the obvious path which now curves left through a third: carry straight on over another big stone stile. The path now runs on the left side of a hedge, passes through the second gateway on the right and then goes diagonally across a field towards the right-hand building in the small hamlet of Carfury. Cross the stile, go through the yard and turn left along the road.

7 At the junction, where there is a small flooded quarry on the right, turn left. *(A few yards beyond the left corner there is a path on the right, starting at a small stile. The path runs south-east past Trythall Farm almost as far as Trythall Vean, and would probably have been part of my recommended route but for the sea of mud I encountered at Trythall Farm. With the aid of an OS map you might care to try it - but obviously I can't tell you what complications you may encounter on the later part of the path.)*
At the crossroads go straight on. Notice the quite large quarry over to the left, in line with the much bigger one at Castle-an-Dinas. Soon there is another stile on the right, but I decided not to try this path because the map shows a more promising-looking alternative. For that, follow the main road round to the right, following the sign to Heamoor and Penzance, and where

*Ding Dong Mine: whim-engine house
St Michael's Mount in the distance*

there is a left bend go straight on along a path between hedges. Where a wider path cuts across, continue ahead, downhill. The path becomes quite narrow again and rather rough underfoot as it descends more steeply into the Chyandour valley. After a few hundred yards on a rather muddy (in January) lane you will reach Kennels Cottage, which I presume takes its name from the fact that the Western Hunt has its headquarters close by. Cross the bridge over the stream and walk up Aldreath road into Madron. A stile on the left near the top of the hill enables you to walk on a footpath which runs beside the road (on the far side of the tall hedge) and gives you a fine view over Mount's Bay. The path continues over three more stiles, but in January the far end was blocked because of building work in progress on new houses; presumably the path will soon be reinstated. If not, you may have to return part of the way in order to get back to the road. On reaching Madron Post Office turn left and right to return to the parking place beside the church.

WALK 8
ZENNOR, GURNARD'S HEAD AND ZENNOR HEAD
WITH POSSIBLE EXTENSIONS

A little over 5 miles, or about 6 if you include Treen.
Round walks of about 1.5 miles and 3 miles are also possible.
The extension to Rosevale Mine would add about a mile.

The Zennor area had comparatively few mines, but there are some unusually interesting sites for the industrial archaeologist on these routes. At Carnelloe are the clifftop remains of a small mine which relied on water power: two big wheel-pits have survived, and the layout of the surface workings of this mine is exceptionally easy to interpret. The ruined engine house of Gurnard's Head Mine is among the most spectacularly-situated of any visited on walks in this book; and in the Foage Valley south-east of Zennor is Rosevale, a small mine which has been lovingly restored to resemble as closely as possible its condition when it was last worked. This is on private land and open to the public only by special arrangement, but several features of it can be seen from the right-of-way nearby. The Wayside Museum in Zennor has a very well presented collection of artefacts related not only to mining but also agriculture and dozens of other rural trades and crafts. I hardly need to point out the magnificence of the scenery on the coastal parts of this walk - more accurately, "these walks", since there is a choice of routes to suit most tastes and abilities. The coast path between Zennor Head and Gurnard's Head is quite tough walking, so don't be deceived by the fairly short distances involved. The pub in Zennor has a name which implies that mining in these parts was once rather more important than I suggested at the start of this note. I remember the Tinners Arms vividly from my first holiday in Cornwall, back in the early '60s: it was there that I tasted a proper pasty for the very first time. Not many others during the 25 years I've actually lived in the Duchy have matched up to that experience! I haven't sampled the pub's food recently, but I'm told it's still very good. There are seasonal toilets at the car park in the village. The pub at Treen, near Gurnard's Head (strictly speaking a hotel, but it has a pub "feel") does outstandingly good food, and is open every day from 11am to about 9.30pm for full meals, teas and other light refreshments. Further mouth-watering details are in the directions. The book to read in connection with this walk and No. 9 is "Tremedda Days": see *TD* in the Bibliography.

ZENNOR

The village takes its name from a saint called Sinar, Sinara or Senara, unknown elsewhere. Most references suggest that the saint was female, and some scholars believe she may be the Breton princess Azenor or Asenora, mother of St Budock. The church's history follows the pattern familiar in Cornwall: a Celtic foundation (probably around 700 AD) whose church was probably mainly of timber; a stone building of the Norman period, much enlarged in the 14th and 15th centuries and heavily restored in the 19th. Old photographs near the organ show something of what the interior looked like before 1890, with box pews and a gallery. The colour guide on sale in the church is attractive and lively but contains little detailed information; it does, however, include the legend of the mermaid and Matthew Trewhella, so I'll leave you to read it there or in one of the many books on Cornish legends and folklore - though, oddly enough, the most famous compilation, Robert Hunt's, gives it no more than the briefest reference. A small notice beside the so-called Mermaid Chair near the pulpit explains the Christian significance of "a mermaid in Church". The carving of the mermaid, "with a comb and a glass in her hand", was originally a bench-end. Under the tower, where the bell ropes are, one of the old slate gravestones commemorates Matthew Thomas, killed in 1809 by a fall of ground at "Wheal Chance on Trewey Downs", an old mine whose workings were close to those of Rosevale. A gravestone outside tells a very different story: Matthew Hollow died at 95, his wife Elizabeth Botterell at 100, and their daughter Elizabeth Uren at 105; Matthew was born in 1816 and his daughter lived till 1949. The sundial on the tower, dating from 1737, was made by Paul Quick, a relative of one of Zennor's best-known figures, the poet (purists say "rhymester") Henry or Henny Quick. The bicentenary of his birth occurred very recently. You can read his verse autobiography in *The Life and Progress of Henry Quick of Zennor,* edited by P. A. S. Pool (Truran, 1984).

> My printed copies then did sell,
> And people seem'd to like them well;
> Parish to parish, town to town,
> I travelled through and sold them round. ......
> Please to take pity on poor Henny,
> I love to gain an honest penny.

The Tinners Arms may have suggested The Tinners' Rest in D. H. Lawrence's story "Samson and Delilah", which tells of a miner who returns from the USA to claim back the wife and daughter he had deserted sixteen years before; the setting of the pub in the story seems to be Pendeen, but Lawrence is said to have written it while staying at the Tinners Arms early in 1916. If you want to go in search of the cottage Lawrence and Frieda later rented, take the path signposted to St Ives (the "Church Road"), on the right just behind the church. After nearly a mile this reaches Tregerthen farm; a minor road to the right from there leads to Higher Tregerthen, where the cottage is. Next door is the "Tower", where Katherine Mansfield and John Middleton Murry lived for a while at the same period. The interesting map in WFWC would be useful in exploring that area. See the comments on Carn Galver Mine's count house (end of section 2 in Walk 6) for further details on this topic.

Directions start at the car park beside a disused chapel a few yards beyond the Wayside Museum in Zennor (*). The village is signposted from the B3306 about 5 miles west of St Ives.

1 *For the shortest walk - a circular tour of Zennor Head - turn left, walk between the church and the pub and take the minor road on your left: there*

THE WAYSIDE MUSEUM

A visit to the little "folk museum" at Zennor is another lively memory that has stayed with me from the holiday I mentioned in my introductory note. It was a very simple and almost primitive affair, despite having been in existence for nearly thirty years even then. Since 1984, when the present owners took over, the buildings have been extensively renovated and the collection has been restored where necessary and greatly enlarged. Most of it is housed in various outbuildings including the old watermill at the end of the garden, where much of the old machinery is still in place, but some rooms in the cottage (originally the miller's house) also contain displays, and other items, including two small waterwheels, are in the open air. "The theme of the Museum," says the excellent Souvenir Guide, " is life in Zennor from 3000 BC to the 1930's." Of special interest to readers of this book (I hope!) will be the mining relics, which include the two waterwheels and also an early set of stamps. One complete room is devoted to a display of pictures, tools and mineral specimens associated with local mining and quarrying. The collection of large-scale maps of the Zennor area, prepared in 1985 for the National Trust, will also be an attraction for walkers, especially if they want to know more about the ancient archaeology of this district. Music lovers may like to know that the Cornish composer George Lloyd, whose works are enjoyed especially by those who do not normally like "modern" music, wrote his opera *Iernin* while living at the mill house, shortly before the Museum was started. Refreshments are available, and there is a shop selling gifts and books. Early in 1993 an estate agent's sign announced that the property was for sale, but I was assured that the future of the Museum is not at risk. Opening times in recent years have been daily from 10am between Easter and the end of October. For up-to-date information phone 0736-796945.

is a footpath sign to Zennor Head. After nearly half a mile you will pass the substantial modern bungalow called Carn Cobba, and then you soon reach the coast path. Continue straight ahead for the headland, picking up the directions at point 5.

For the main walk, turn right on leaving the car park, walk back past the Wayside Museum (*) to Trewey Farm, at the main road, and there take the signposted public footpath on the right. For a few yards you are on a farm track - muddy in January - and then you cross the first of several "stiles" that might better be called granite cattle-grids. ("Cornish stiles", they are called in these parts.) The grassy path runs between hedges at first, then follows the hedge on the right. The course of the path is mostly clear, heading in a fairly straight line towards the rocky ridge of Carn Galver. The seventh stile (just in case you've been counting) is beside a gateway at the corner of a field; the path then runs beside a hedge on the right, and after one more stile joins a track running beside a group of cottages at Poniou, "bridges".

2 Just before the track reaches the main road, turn right on to another track heading for the coast. (There is a public footpath sign beside the road.) Keep to the main track as it curves right, and go through the wooden farm gate beside a stream. At this point you get your first good view of Gurnard's Head, but don't let that distract you from noticing the big wheelpit (colour photo. 25) down on the left as you approach the bungalow. All around you now are relics of a small mine called Carnelloe or Zennor Consols (*). I had a long chat with the owner of the bungalow, and promised him I would stress that all these relics are on private land. Most of them can be seen quite well from the paths, and there is no reason to go clambering about on and among them - an activity which has caused considerable damage to some features as well as being distinctly risky. The bungalow itself is a relic of the mine, since it was used as its count house - and I was told there have even been some

---

CARNELLOE MINE OR ZENNOR CONSOLS

Zennor Consols was a group formed in 1851, "consolidating" several old mines including Zennor Head Mine and Carnelloe (sometimes spelt "Carnella" or "Carnellow"). Few if any records seem to exist of how that venture fared, but MC1 and MMC refer to the work in progress at Carnelloe in 1862, when the mine apparently depended completely on water power. A 42-ft. waterwheel was used for winding and to drive twelve heads of stamps. Another company took over in 1872 and sank a new shaft named Engine Shaft. That might seem to imply the use of steam, but it was the normal name in Cornwall for any shaft containing pitwork, however it was driven: steam, horse or water. A "water engine" rather than a "fire engine" was used here: the new company bought a 37-ft. waterwheel for pumping and an iron waterwheel to drive eight heads of stamps and also haul up a tramway attached to the face of the cliff. The mine closed in 1876 despite very optimistic assessments by miners of its prospects. "This little mine produced slabs of almost clean cassiterite," says Jenkin, but the only recorded output is 6 tons of black tin in 1872-3 (MMR). Justin Brooke, who supplied several of the foregoing details, also told me that an ambitious plan to re-open Carnelloe Mine as recently as 1964 was abandoned only for legal reasons.

---

passers-by who have roamed around the building peering through the windows! The owner told me that the original workings of the mine were on the higher ground inland (the OS Pathfinder map indicates "Shafts" a short way east, of Carnelloe), and he believes that the earliest dressing floors were up there. (Dines in <u>MMR</u> identifies these inland workings as probably those of a small mine called Wheal Dollar; this was working with Carnelloe during the 1830s.) Later, a reservoir was built nearer the cliffs - one wall of it can be seen up on your right just above the upper wheelpit - and water to power the two big wheels was brought to it by a leat from the stream you have just crossed. The first waterwheel did two jobs: it wound from the shaft down by the cliff-edge, hauling the tin-stuff up to this level by means of a short tramway, and it operated the stamps. Hidden by the low scrub on the right of the wheelpit are small dressing floors including buddles. Justin Brooke tells me that a slag-heap was found nearby, suggesting that the mine also had its own blowing house (for smelting) at one period. According to <u>TD</u> the smelting works was on the east side of Carnelloe headland, and the crushed and buddled ore was taken there in panniers or donkey-carts. Continue down the path, which runs to the right of the bungalow (what a superb view, in both directions!) and then steeply down to join the coast path.

3 *Here turn right, picking up the directions at point 4, if you prefer not to include the diversion to Gurnard's Head - but first it would be worth going a few yards left to see other features of Carnelloe mine.*
For Gurnard's Head turn left, past the lower wheelpit, which is surrounded by several gunnises (surface workings); the shaft from which the waterwheel pumped, now choked at surface, is, I understand, on the seaward side of the wheelpit. The path approaching the stream, which ends as a waterfall at Porthglaze Cove, is steep, wet and rather rough in places, but beyond the footbridge things improve. This stretch of coast, called Boswednack Cliff, is National Trust property, as is Gurnard's Head. Look back to get a clear view of one of the stopes beside the lower wheelpit. Near the tip of the closest headland, Carn Nean Point, are, I'm told, the remains of a horse-whim plat which was employed, along with a 30" beam engine for pumping from two shafts, by a mine called North United during the 1840s. Rather strangely, there seem to be no traces of mine dumps in that area. Soon comes another bridge over a rushing stream, and presumably this one supplied power to the nearby Gurnard's Head Mine (*), in addition to the steam engine it invested

---

GURNARD'S HEAD MINE
The earliest recorded mining venture here was the Treen Copper Mine, which started before 1821 and had sunk its main shaft on a small rocky headland where a ten-foot-high wall was required to keep the sea out at spring high tides. By 1837, when the name Gurnard's or Gurnett's Head Mine was in use, the main shaft had reached a depth of nearly 250 feet below sea level, and a report quoted in <u>MMC</u> implies that the mine was still relying entirely on water power then. A 40ft. waterwheel was being used for pumping at that time. Collins states that it employed 24 people at this time (<u>WEMR</u>). A new company took over in 1843, but this lasted only till 1847, despite some good finds of copper. The engine house, built for a 30" pumping engine, apparently belongs to this period.

in for pumping. The coast path crosses a wider track and continues ahead, up beside the engine house (colour photo. 24), the bob wall of which is perched precariously on the lip of an open shaft. Down beside the edge of the cliff is a ruined building, now partly adapted as a woodshed. It looks like a relic of the mine, but could perhaps have been associated with what Cyril Noall describes as the "curious little pilchard seining fishery at Gurnard's Head" (CSS) which had a wooden landing stage beneath the sheer cliffs at Treen Cove during the latter half of last century.

Having come this far it would be a pity not to extend the walk to Gurnard's Head (*) itself, from which the views are magnificent. On the right side of the coast path about a quarter of a mile beyond the engine house - just before quite a steep climb - are the foundations of what the OS map calls Chapel Jane (*). (Colour photo. 26)

Gurnard's Head Mine, probably about 1890, more than 40 years after the mine closed. The stack is now just a stump. The other building may have been connected with the mine, but seems to have been converted into a dwelling by this time. Beside the road in the foreground is some of the photographer's equipment, including an umbrella or sunshade and a portable developer.

GURNARD'S HEAD

Its modern name is said to allude to the supposed resemblance of the promontory to the fish; a century or more ago the normal version was "Gurnett's Head", "gurnet" being an alternative name for a gurnard. Its old name is Izner, possibly derived from Cornish *ynyal* ("wild, desolate"), and the maps also label it Trereen Dinas, from Cornish *tre-dyn dynas,* "farm of the fort fort". (The "farm of the fort" is, of course, Treen; there is another Treen near the Minack Theatre, and that stands beside a headland called Treryn Dinas.) Like almost every other high Cornish headland, this one was fortified during the Iron Age. Two ramparts and three ditches can still be traced across the neck; the inner wall is of masonry and seems to be equipped with three steps from which the defenders could aim their slingshots. Archaeologists in 1939 detected the foundations of 16 round houses, each about 20-30 feet in diameter. All these remains are thought to date from about 200 BC. Francis Kilvert wrote a vivid account of a visit to Gurnard's Head in 1870: "I wandered round the cliffs to the broken rocks at the furthest point of the Head, and sat alone amongst the wilderness of broken shattered tumbled cliffs, listening to the booming and breaking of the waves below and watching the flying skirts of the showers of spray. Perfect solitude." (KCD)

CHAPEL JANE

An excavation carried out here in 1964-6 was the subject of an interesting article in "Cornish Archaeology" No. 7 (1968). The authors, Vivien Russell and P. A. S. Pool, concluded that this little building probably was indeed a chapel, likely to have been used between about 1100 and 1500. Among the objects found was a "mensa" or altar table, rather similar to the one at Madron Baptistry (Walk 7), upon which the priest would probably have placed a portable altar. Nearby is or was a Holy Well credited with great healing powers, but the exact site of that is very doubtful; it may have been destroyed by cliff erosion. There is in fact a small natural spring some 18 feet to the south, just below the cliff edge. The name "Chapel Jane" was supposed to have been first used by the early-18th-century historian William Hals, who explained it as meaning "narrow chapel". That is certainly apt, but Russell and Pool believe Hals actually wrote "Idne" or "Jelne", and that he intended "Chapel Innyall" or "Ynyal", which as mentioned elsewhere may have been an old name for Gurnard's Head. A document of 1580 referred to the building as "Innyall Chapel". Dr C. A. Ralegh Radford has suggested that that it may have been built here to serve the needs of the fishermen based at Treen Cove: not just their spiritual needs (prayers for good catches, safe return, and so on), but also their physical safety, since there is some evidence of a small tower at the western end of the building where a guiding light may have been placed.

4 Not far past that, fork right for the headland. Eventually return to Carnelloe by the same route unless you want to include the following diversion, which would add rather less than a mile to the walk.

From Gurnard's Head there is a path inland to the hamlet of Treen, where you could get refreshments at the Gurnard's Head Hotel. For that, return along the same path at first, but don't fork left, and when you reach the coast path continue straight ahead uphill, through bracken. Keep to the main path as it winds up to the top of the hill; from there it runs in a fairly straight line, crossing three large granite stiles before reaching Treen, where there are two smaller stiles. On the right are coastguard cottages, one bearing a George VI emblem. Continue to the main road for the Hotel, which has on offer an amazing range of dishes at what we thought very reasonable prices. In deference to the setting we chose "Smoked Gurnard Crumble", and it lived up to the description: "Locally smoked gurnard cooked in a rich creamy onion sauce with a little chopped egg, covered with cheese and a crunchy crumble topping, served with fresh vegetables." I followed that with "Thunder and Lightning", which included ice cream, black treacle, clotted cream and gin.... Luckily our car was parked outside, and we decided against that walk on Zennor Hill! If you have a walk to complete, the easiest thing to do (when you're sufficiently recovered) is return to the coast path by the same route. There is a shorter way which would bring you to the coast at Gurnard's Head Mine, but the path is badly maintained. If you want to try it, take the track which curves right as it leaves Treen: there is a metal gate with a rudimentary stile beside it. After about 50 yards there is a stile on the left, but this had barbed wire across it so we used the nearby gateway. Now you need to head slightly left of the nearest house. After crossing a boggy patch near a concreted well we climbed a lowish wall, crossed a smallish stream, ducked under some barbed wire ... and from there the path was clear, running down towards the lower house. A few narrow planks gave some help in crossing another wet patch. The path runs to the right behind the house and brings you to a surfaced lane; go left on that, and soon you reach the coast path just west of the engine house. Turn right for Carnelloe and Zennor.

At Carnelloe follow the signs indicating the coast path and Zennor. On the east side of the headland you have quite a strenuous climb above Veor Cove. ("Veor" is derived from the Cornish word for "big", so "Veor Cove" means the same as "Porthmeor" nearby and also "Porthbeor" in the Roseland.) A mine called Wheal Veor (a very small mine, despite its name!) is mentioned in TD; Alison Symons refers to the horse whim it employed, and says its "central stone, with a hole in the middle, is still visible, as is the small shelter hewn out of solid rock where the young lad, who kept the horse moving, could sit protected from the westerly gales." Nearby was the smelting works I mentioned earlier. After Veor Cove the path runs fairly level above the gently sloping cliffs, out of which rise great rocky stacks, before making a descent above Pendour ("head of the water") Cove, famous for its association with the legendary Zennor mermaid. A seat at the top of the slope gives a good opportunity to study the massive headland, cut into by a deep, narrow cleft known as Horseback Zawn from the shape of the ridge that divides it from the sea; and also the valley, where the ruins of an old watermill are overshadowed by the modern bungalow ("Carn Cobba") that looks so out of place in this setting. Eglosmeor (Great Church) Mill, referred to in TD as Steven's Mill, was destroyed by the flood of 12th November 1894 which did so much damage in local mines such as Wheal Cock (Botallack) - and see the contemporary photograph of Tregenna Hill in St Ives (page 48 in

SIH). A battery of stamps was also sited close to the mill at one time. As you walk down towards the stream there is a glimpse of Zennor church. A footbridge provides a fine view of what in winter was a torrent roaring around and over massive granite boulders. Then comes a long climb up a flight of steps, with a welcome seat part-way up, ending at a T-junction where you could turn right for Zennor or complete the recommended walk by turning left for Zennor Head.

5 Fixed to the rocky outcrop above the tip of the headland is a plaque giving some information about the presentation of this place to the National Trust in 1953. A little further on there is a second such outcrop, and beside that what looks like evidence of an early mining venture, a long, shallow trench running inland from near the cliff edge. Much of the ground around this spot seems to have been disturbed in a way characteristic of many small-scale shallow workings. The path now descends and climbs again on the eastern side of the headland, and just before it reaches a level path at the top, where there is a coast-path signpost, any doubts that this area has been mined are dispelled by the water-filled portal of an adit beside the path. According to NT10, in fact, the lower cliffs here are "riddled with adits" of tin and copper mines.

6 Turn right at the coast path sign to return to Zennor by the high path. Keep to the main path as it wanders among bracken and low scrub, and at the T-junction turn left on the wider path. After crossing a stile above the big bungalow, Carn Cobba, you are on a narrow road into Zennor. Keep straight on after passing the church to return to the car park.

By the way, if you are tempted to try to walk to the so-called Giant's Rock just north of Zennor, as recommended by Donald Vage in one of his books of walks, please be warned that you will have to battle through thick gorse or clamber over huge boulders to reach it. We gave up the attempt.

A POSSIBLE SHORT EXTENSION
TO ROSEVALE MINE
with the further option of a walk on
ZENNOR HILL

If you are interested in having a look - albeit a fairly distant one - at Rosevale Mine (*) (about half a mile away), with or without doing another complete round walk, take the road going left from the church. At the main road turn right, and after a few yards left on to the lane which goes up the valley to Rosemorran and Foage Farm. The Zennor stream runs close to the lane, on the right. Rosevale Mine can be seen on the same side, just north of Rosemorran. The foundations of the stamp base and the stone walls of the extensive dressing floors are clearly visible close to the stream. The entrance to the lower level of the mine (colour photo. 28) is near the sheds and the upper level entrance lies above this, half-way up the hillside. The line of small

stone walls running up the hill supported a tramline which fed the stamps from the upper level. (In addition to the "boxed note" on Rosevale, you may care to read what Alison Symons has to say about it in TD. Her father was working there as a boy of 16 at the time of its closure in 1913.)
Please note: the mine is on private land, and is not accessible to the public without prior permission from the owners. Underground tours of the mine are available by pre-arrangement but, at present, only to groups of 10-15 people at a time. These tours are arranged through Peninsula Mining Company Ltd and further details can be obtained by phoning the company on (0736) 740618.

ROSEVALE MINE
(Note kindly supplied by Tony Bennett)
Also called Rosemorran, this was a small mine which worked shallow lodes by means of adits driven into the hillside. Most of the work was concentrated on one lode - called the Red Lode - which was developed for a length of about 1000 feet by two levels. Little has been recorded of its history, but it was never a very rich mine. It probably started late in the 18th century and continued intermittently during the 19th. It was worked by local miners from 1906 to 1912 and was then taken over by Rayfield Tin Syndicate Ltd. 36 people were employed and an extensive dressing floor was constructed, including six head of Californian stamps; the machinery used to be driven by water power and later by a gas engine. This operation ceased in 1913. In 1974 the West Cornwall Mining & Minerals Club leased the property and started to renovate the underground workings on the main lode. Shortly after this the club was wound up but two of its members carried on activities at the mine. Nowadays the mine is leased by the Rosevale Historical Mining Society, consisting of Mike Shipp (who was a founder member of the original group) and Tony Bennett, who continue to restore and preserve the workings as a traditional Cornish mine. The work is performed as a weekend hobby "for the sheer joy of it". They have cleared most of the main tunnels, renovated the timberwork, re-equipped the mine with authentic mining equipment and relics and installed a ladderway through a narrow vertical stope to link the upper and lower levels. The task is very much on-going and there is still much work to be done!

If you would like to extend this short expedition, you might try the round walk on Zennor Hill laid out by the National Trust, which can be further extended to include Zennor Quoit. To do that, continue up the valley road for about another quarter of a mile. The NT path is signposted on the left, not far beyond Sener Cottage, and before the lane reaches Foage Farm. A few lines of guidance on the route of this walk are included in NT10. I apologise for the fact that I haven't tried it myself: blame the good food at the Gurnard's Head Hotel!

WALK 9
HALSETOWN CHURCH, TREVAIL, RIVER COVE AND THE CLIFFS

Nearly 6 miles

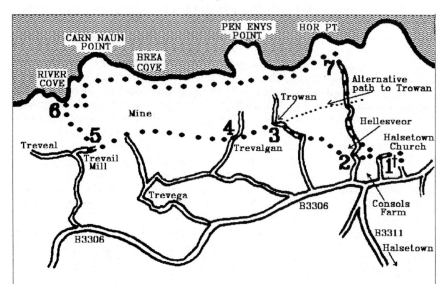

This walk divides fairly equally into two very contrasting parts: field paths through quite flat farmland with fine inland views of the hills from Rosewall to Carn Galver, and a much more strenuous clifftop walk with equally fine coastal views, especially to the east. Between the two is a very attractive and unspoilt valley running down to the sea. The route passes through or close to the setts of at least five mines: one described by A. K. Hamilton Jenkin as "rich and important", two medium-sized enterprises and two that scarcely seem to have got properly under way. In January this was definitely a walk to take your wellies on: cattle had churned up most gateways and many of the farm lanes into sticky mud at least ankle-deep; some of the farms seemed to be having a bumper slurry-making season; and even on the coast path there were some very boggy stretches. Things may be very different in July, but I wouldn't bank on it. Ideally, take a good stout pair of walking boots too, because this is in general a pretty rough and rocky part of the coast. A stick would also be useful to help with a few awkward, perhaps overgrown stiles and one or two low walls that may need to be climbed near the start. There is no pub or shop along the way.

HALSETOWN CHURCH, ST JOHN'S-IN-THE-FIELDS ,

An outline of the story of how Halsetown (say "Hallstown") came to be created at the time of the 1832 electoral reform act is given in *A View from Trencrom;* if you have not, as they say, "invested" in that, read the very detailed history of St John's on sale in the church, which not only tells the story but adds human flesh to the bare bones. Several of the mines nearby, such as St Ives Consols and Giew, had a large and expanding work force during the second quarter of the 19th century, so the need for an Anglican church closer than St Ives came increasingly to be felt. Permission for Halsetown, with the addition of nearby hamlets such as Hellesvean and Hellesveor, to be constituted a separate parish was granted in 1846. The obvious choice of architect for the new church and vicarage was J. P. St Aubyn, who seems to have played a leading part in the "restoration" of almost every medieval church in Cornwall, much to the disgust of Sir John Betjeman and others. Even Betjeman, however, found St John's "impressive" - certainly it is distinctive, and manages to feel spacious yet friendly inside, though the friendliness is partly a result of decisions within the last twenty years to remove the pews and pulpit, carpet the entire floor and move the altar to a central position. Why build the church so far from the village? The reason is said to be that all the landowners there were "chapel" and no-one would sell land to the Anglicans! And what about the fields? In fact the site chosen was indeed very rural at the time. St Ives has expanded to enclose it, and has shifted its centre of gravity in this direction to such an extent that Halsetown parish now has a larger population than St Ives.

There is a large car park at Halsetown church (*) - which, please note, is NOT in Halsetown! To drive to it, take the St Just / Land's End road out of St Ives (B3306). As you approach the edge of the town you will see the church, with its distinctive gabled spire (is that the word for it?), on your right, and the side road leading to it comes about a quarter of a mile before the junction with the Penzance road (B3311).

1 The path runs behind the church car park: access to it is at the right-hand corner, up a few steps and under a low arch. Turn left on the path, which soon brings you to a pretty group of cottages. Continue almost straight ahead, following a footpath sign, beside one of the cottages. A few steps lead up into a field. (A short way to the left now is Consols Farm. The farm house was formerly the count house of one of the major mines of this area, St Ives Consols (*).) Here turn right, keep to the field-edge for a few yards, then follow the obvious path diagonally across the field, and when you reach the hedge cross the stile ahead.

(NOTE: the field path between here and Trowan Farm is not well maintained, and if you feel reluctant to climb gates and scramble over awkward stiles or walls you might prefer to try a longer but more frequently used alternative. For that, don't cross the stile but continue with the hedge on your left, through a kissing-gate and then a small metal gate where there are steps down to a farm track. After about a quarter of a mile on that, cross the stile on the left, where there is a footpath sign to Zennor. The path -

ST IVES CONSOLS

"Then we came to a mine called St Ives Consols, and the works, rattling, clanking, clumping, at 'stamping' and streaming' tin." So wrote Francis Kilvert in his diary on 29th July, 1870 (KCD). Five years earlier, Thomas Spargo had noted, "The late Mr James Halse made a fortune out of this mine." It was easily the most productive one in the area explored on this walk: Collins (WEMR) estimates the value of the tin and copper raised between 1827 and 1892 as just over a million pounds, and states that for most of this period the mine employed between 300 and 500 people. An unusual feature of the mine was the so-called "carbonas", great irregular masses of tin ore. The largest, at a depth of 77 fathoms below adit, when extracted left caverns as much as 70 feet in height and width. These caverns had to be supported with, as Cyril Noall puts it in CMD, "absolute forests" of wooden beams and pillars, and the mine suffered a considerable blow in 1844 when the supports in the Great Carbona were accidentally set alight through the carelessness of a miner who left his candle stuck to one of the roof timbers. The fire burnt on for six weeks. The mine, under various names, had a long life: Hamilton Jenkin (MMC) writes of its being "re-started" in 1818 - and its final "re-start" was 90 years later, when a new company operated it in conjunction with three neighbouring mines: Rosewall Hill and Ransome United, Trenwith and Giew. This operation ceased in 1915 in the original St Ives Consols section, but continued till 1923 at Giew, whose big pumping-engine house at Frank's Shaft still dominates the countryside near the Engine Inn at Cripplesease. Walks visiting the Rosewall mines and Giew are included in *A View from Trencrom.* A larger version of the 1860s photograph is in Lena and Donald Bray's *St Ives Heritage* (1981; revised edition 1992, Landfall Publications), which also includes interesting personal reminiscences connected with mining in the St Ives area early this century.

which is, in fact, the "Church Road" mentioned in point 3 of Walk 6 - is shown on the maps as running in a fairly straight line to Trowan Farm. I have not walked it, but I suspect that posts painted black and white have been set up at strategic points along the way. Pick up the directions at point 3.)
For the more direct route, continue roughly in the same line and cross the stile just left of Hellesveor farmhouse. A very sticky patch comes next; negotiate that, go through the gateway and continue ahead along the minor road among the farm buildings and houses of Hellesveor hamlet. (The name derives from Cornish words meaning "ancient court" or "old ruins", with the addition of "veor", large. The "old ruins" may be "the Dark-Age building excavated at Hellesvean" (CPE).)

2 Turn left after a few yards, passing a house and a cowshed on your left, and take the path running between hedges, which starts on the right of a farm gate and will probably have a metal bar across it. Look left to see Knill's Steeple in the distance, Trink Hill further right with the big engine house of Giew Mine on its right, and Rosewall Hill closer - recognisable by the two mine stacks on its left-hand slope. We soon came to a gate which proved easier to climb than to untie. When you enter an open field, continue in the same line. The chimney quite close now on your left is a relic of St Ives Wheal

Allen (*). I believe there ought to be a stile in the left-hand corner of the field, but since it has gone you need to pass through the gateway further right, then turn left and go through the gate there. Now head slightly right, walking almost to the far end of this fairly long field. Again there is no proper stile, but a little way past the metal farm gate on the right a large boulder in the hedge marks a point where climbing is quite easy. Make for the nearest farm. There is a narrow, rather overgrown stile in the thorn hedge ahead; after

This famous photograph by Gibson of dressing floors at St Ives Consols mine is said to date from about 1863. The mine was at the height of its success then: Thomas Spargo in "The Mines of Cornwall" (1865) stated, "it is now the favourite mine, both far and near, as a security for money." He reported that it was currently operating five steam engines and five water-stamping mills and had a workforce consisting of 218 men, 59 females and 104 boys. The majority of the workers in this picture seem to be women and children, all of them carefully posed by the photographer. The stack in the background suggests that these dressing floors were beside the steam stamps, opposite the count house, now Consols Farm.

ST IVES WHEAL ALLEN

Although Collins suggests that the original name of this tin mine may have been Wheal Ellen (WEMR), Dr Hamilton Jenkin mentions a tradition that it was worked by a St Ives family called Allen in the 1730s (MMC). He also quotes from a document dated 1786 which refers to the workings of Wheal Allen as already "old". During the following century the mine invested in steam engines for pumping and stamping, but it relied entirely on horses for winding, like so many smaller, shallow concerns. Dr Jenkin paints a vivid picture of the two horses at each of the three whims as they "plodded round and round the whim plats almost without attention, the boy drivers sitting half asleep on the capstan bars". St Ives Wheal Allen appears to have closed in 1868: its machinery was advertised for sale in the *West Briton* on 23rd April. Little if anything remains on the surface to tell of this mine's existence save the lonely stack, from a 30" pumping engine; there is still less to be seen of another old mine which was its close neighbour and seems to have been more productive in its latter years: Goole Pellas Mine, whose sett was on the other side of the main road, just a little further west.

negotiating that, cross the narrow field to another stile - much less awkward, but rather tumbledown - and continue along the lane to Trowan Farm.

3 The path to Zennor - the "Church Road" again - is clearly signed, to the left of the farmhouse. You have two stiles to cross within a few yards, each of which has a post painted black and white beside it. From here to Trevalgan Farm the path runs quite straight; there are five more stiles, the last of them just to the right of the farm buildings, and every stile but one has a painted post nearby. (Even the one exception has the remains of a post.)

4 Just beyond the farmhouse there are two stiles side-by-side; cross the right-hand one, where there is (or was) a sign, Public Footpath to Trevail. Keep by the hedge on your left as it curves right, and go through the second gateway on your left. Now head slightly right of the stamps-engine house of Trevega Bal (*), cutting off the left-hand corner of the field, and cross the stile just beyond the point where the stone hedge juts out. Now walk with the hedge on your left (the engine house should be straight ahead now), crossing two more stiles. The second, just left of a metal gate, is awkward to climb down on the far side. By now the view ahead is just beginning to reveal Carn Galver, emerging from behind Zennor Hill; and to your left between Rosewall and Trendrine Hills is the valley in which Towednack church is situated. Unsurprisingly, since it has a very low tower, we did not notice it from this distance. The path goes on in the same line with the hedge now on your right, crossing six more stiles, the last of which brings you to a lane. Here turn right and then almost immediately left. (According to the maps there ought to be three public footpaths starting near this point, one of which goes to the coast and the others to the disused mine, but all of them seem to be securely fenced off and/or completely overgrown. I shall make enquiries and hope to get some if not all of them reinstated. No harm in hoping ...!) The path to Trevail Mill, down in the valley, from here on is very clear. At the point where you cross the stream there is a pond to the right - presumably the original mill pond. NT10 states that there were originally two mills at Trevail. The

---

TREVEGA BAL

This mine appears in the records of Cornish mining under various names, such as Trevega and Brea Mines, Brea Tin Mine, Brea Consols and West St Ives Consols; and before any of these groups were formed there were five independent enterprises known as Wheals Brea, Fat, Richards, Matthews and Parkis. ("Wheal Fat" is a fairly common mine name in Cornwall, applied where rich tin deposits were found at or near the surface.) Some if not all of them were very old: the use of gunpowder for blasting in West Penwith is said to have been pioneered here as early as 1700, and Fat and Brea were making good profits on tin sales in 1779-80. As the mine developed during the 19th century, the deepest workings were near the cliffs and under the sea at Brea Cove. It closed in 1871; according to MMC it was "last investigated, in a half-hearted way, immediately prior to the 1914 war." Alison Symons in TD gives some details about work carried out during the first two decades of this century at "Trevail Mine", by which I presume this one is meant. The "dirt" from the mine was drawn up by a "whipsaderry", that is a Whip-and-Derry (= derrick), defined as "A kibble drawn to the surface by a horse, the rope attaching one to the other, and simply passing over a pulley" (GMT). It was then carted to the other side of the valley where there were water-powered stamps, but in the mine's last years the cart was replaced by an overhead cable system operated by a steam engine.

---

attractive mill house that stands there now was being extensively renovated when we did this walk. The path runs right beside it and then starts to climb towards Treveal - now basically a farm, but in the great days of mining it "would have been a vigorous and well-populated hamlet" (NT10).

5 A few yards beyond the mill house there is a small path on the right, leading down the valley. You could take that, or go a little further up the concreted drive to the more definite path, where there is a NT sign, River Cove. The two paths soon merge. The top part of the Treveal Valley is quite thickly wooded. Among the trees and down by the stream there are several small excavations and one deeper hole that looks very much like an adit. Some of these features may have been created by Trevega Bal, but most are probably evidence of a much smaller concern called Wheal Cleveland, dating from the 1840s - "little more than a trial" according to MMR. Soon the trees come to an end, and a beautiful view of the little valley opens up. It looks about as remote from industrial landscape as can be imagined, but the nearby mines made full use of the Treveal stream to drive stamps and supply buddles. Continue ahead on the path down the western side of the valley till you reach the coast path near the cliff edge.

6 Turn right on that. It winds down to the valley bottom, where there is a stone footbridge. The side path to the rocks overlooking River Cove is worth a short diversion: this is often a good vantage point for watching seals. The long depression that starts as the Trevail Valley and the gap between Rosewall and Trendrine Hills continues as the Red River Valley via Towednack, Nancledra and Crowlas almost as far as Marazion, so that from a few miles out to sea it appears that all the land to the west is an island: C.

Lewis Hind in *Days in Cornwall* (1907) writes that seamen call River Cove "the Open Gate". The coast path itself now takes you on a long climb up to the top of Treveal Cliff, above Carn Naun Point - an exceptionally bare, bleak spot, but what a view it commands! Pendeen Watch (about 7 miles) cuts off the view south-west, but once you reach the trig. point column you can look east to Godrevy lighthouse (about 6.5 m.), St Agnes Beacon (just over 13 m.), Kelsey Head near Newquay (c. 22 m.) and in clear conditions Trevose Head near Padstow (c. 32 m.). Quite close at hand is the Trevega stamps-engine house, and when you reach the rocky outcrop above Brea Cove you will be able to see another ruined mine building part-way down the sloping cliff. This was a pumping-engine house, and the mouth of the shaft from which it pumped is probably on the flat area just below it. (Colour photo. 29) At the bottom of the cliff, just above high-water mark, are the portals of "several adits" according to Barry Atkinson (MSC); the same mine also had a much longer adit - nearly half a mile - which drained into the sea at River Cove. The next big headland is Pen Enys ("Island Head") Point; before reaching that the path runs close to the head of the impressive zawn called Polgassick Cove, where wooden duckboarding and concrete paving slabs have been laid down to help you across one of the many boggy patches on this stretch of cliff. "Polgassick" means "mare's pool"; certainly there's plenty of water to take the horse to up here! Beyond a kissing gate the path crosses two streams as it cuts across the neck of the headland. Ahead now is Hor ("Ram") Point - which may take you longer to reach than you expect, since this part of the cliff path is particularly rough underfoot. The coast path again runs well inland of the point itself, but there is a clear path out to it on the far (eastern) side, and this is well worth the diversion if old mines interest you. Hor copper mine occupies only the tiniest of niches in mining history, but it has left a massive shaft (blocked a few feet down) in a very spectacular situation. The base of a masonry wall rests precariously on the edge of the shaft, with fallen blocks scattered among the mine waste nearby (colour photo. 30). A note in A. K. Hamilton Jenkin's *The Cornish Miner* (1927) mentions "Captain Martin Dunn's engine-house at Hor Bal". Old people could remember that 16 horses had to be used to manoeuvre the bob along the twisting, narrow lane. "It took several days to get it down, and all the neighbourhood turned out to see it." Just above the shaft is a circular "plat" about 35 feet in diameter, possibly the site of a horse whim. Des Hannigan in NT10 tells the story of how in 1957 the National Trust and the owner of Hor Point combined to foil a plan by St Ives Town Council to purchase the headland compulsorily and turn it into a garbage tip. Continue on the coast path till you reach a sign indicating St Ives to the left; close by is the National Trust Hellesveor Cliff sign.

7 Here leave the coast path, continuing ahead along a farm lane or track between hedges. After about a quarter of a mile there is a wooden gate, and soon after that the main inland path between Zennor and St Ives crosses. Roughly the same distance again brings you to a house (Pedn-an-Vounder), and not far beyond that the track turns quite sharply to the right. At that point, go through the small metal gate up on the left. Walk beside the hedge on your right, through a kissing-gate, a few more yards beside the hedge and then diagonally left across the field. The path on your left beside a house soon returns you to St John's-in-the-Fields.

USING PUBLIC TRANSPORT

WALKS 1 - 5
Some information about buses to and from St Just and St Ives is included in the introduction to the ST JUST MINES TRAIL, page 8. The B3306 between Portherras Cross and St Just is also served by buses to and from Penzance.

WALKS 6, 8 AND 9
There is a summertime service between St Just and St Ives, calling at Morvah, the Gurnard's Head Hotel and Zennor, but it runs only twice per day in each direction, and not at all on Saturdays. A Hoppa from the centre of St Ives would get you near the start of Walk 9.

WALK 7
Hoppas run between Penzance and Madron. Western National provides one bus per day (not Sundays) from St Just to Penzance via Madron in the morning, returning in the afternoon.

PLEASE NOTE
The above information may well be out of date by the time you use this book. Please consult current timetables.

A reminder of Walk 6.
Coffee stop on a January morning - and a chance to enjoy
a view from Carn Galver!

BIBLIOGRAPHY

The following publications are referred to in the directions and boxed notes, using the abbreviations given on the left.

ASDC T. Clare: *Archaeological Sites of Devon and Cornwall* (Moorland, 1982)

CAH Nicholas Johnson and Peter Rose: *Cornwall's Archaeological Heritage* (Twelveheads, 1990)

CAU Adam Sharpe: *St Just - An Archaeological Survey of the Mining District* (2 volumes) (Cornwall Archaeological Unit, 1992)

CEH H. G. Ordish: *Cornish Engine-Houses, A Second Pictorial Survey* (D. Bradford Barton, 1968)

CHN Charles Henderson: Notes on the 109 ancient parishes of the Four Western Hundreds of Cornwall (1910-24), published in the Journal of the Royal Institution of Cornwall, 1955-60

CMD Cyril Noall: *Cornish Mine Disasters* (Truran, 1989)

CMM J. R. Leifchild: *Cornwall, Its Mines and Miners* (1855. Reprinted by Frank Cass & Co., 1968)

CMS J. H. Trounson: *Historic Cornish Mining Scenes at Surface* (D. Bradford Barton, 1968)

CNB Cyril Noall: *Botallack* (D. Bradford Barton, 1972)

CNG Cyril Noall: *Geevor* (Geevor Tin Mines plc, 1983)

CNL Cyril Noall: *Levant - The Mine beneath the Sea* (D. B. Barton, 1970)

CNSI Cyril Noall: *The St Ives Mining District,* Vol. One (Truran, 1982)

CNSJ Cyril Noall: *The St Just Mining District* (D. Bradford Barton, 1973)

CPE Oliver J. Padel: *Cornish Place-Name Elements* (English Place-Name Society, 1985)

CPN Oliver J. Padel: *A Popular Dictionary of Cornish Place-Names* (Alison Hodge, 1988)

CSS Cyril Noall: *Cornish Seines and Seiners* (D. Bradford Barton, 1972)

CWB Craig Weatherhill: *Belerion: Ancient Sites of Land's End* (Alison Hodge, 1981)

CWC Craig Weatherhill: *Cornovia: Ancient Sites of Cornwall & Scilly* (Alison Hodge, 1985)

EBT "Edward Bosanketh" (Richard Edward Boyns): *Tin, A Novel* (1888. New edition published by Justin Brooke, 1988.)

ECMH1/2 D. B. Barton: *Essays in Cornish Mining History,* Vols. 1 & 2 (Bradford Barton, 1968 & 1971)

GM J. A. Buckley: *Geevor Mine* (Geevor Tourist Amenity, 1989)

GMT (Ed.) W. G. Orchard: *A Glossary of Mining Terms* (Truran, 1990)

HWC A. Lane-Davies: *Holy Wells of Cornwall* (Federation of Old Cornwall Societies, 1970)

HWCCC P. O. & D. V. Leggat: *The Healing Wells: Cornish Cults and Customs* (Truran, 1987)

JTS Ian Cooke: *Journey to the Stones* (Men-an-Tol Studio, 1987)

KCD ed. Richard Maber and Angela Tregoning: *Kilvert's Cornish Diary* (Alison Hodge, 1989)

LCCM John Corin: *Levant - A Champion Cornish Mine*
(Trevithick Society, 1992)

MC   William Pryce: *Mineralogia Cornubiensis* (1778, reprinted 1972 by
D. Bradford Barton)

MC1   Thomas Spargo: *The Mines of Cornwall, 1: The Land's End
Peninsula* (1865, reprinted by D. Bradford Barton, 1959)

MIC   J. H. Trounson : *Mining in Cornwall, 1850-1960,* Volume Two
(Moorland, 1982)

MMC A. K. Hamilton Jenkin: *Mines and Miners of Cornwall, 1. Around
St Ives* (1961. Reprinted by Forge Books, 1978)

MMP Henry R. Jennings: *Notes on the History of Madron, Morvah and
Penzance* (1936)

MMR H. G. Dines: *The Metalliferous Mining Region of South-West
England* (2 volumes) (HMSO, 1956)

MSC   Barry Atkinson: *Mining Sites in Cornwall and South West Devon*
(Truran, 1988)

MUS   "Jack Penhale" (Raymond Harry): *The Mine under the Sea*
(J. H. Lake, 1962)

NT10 National Trust "Coast of Cornwall" leaflet No. 10: West Penwith
- St Ives to Pendeen

NT11 National Trust "Coast of Cornwall" leaflet No. 11: West Penwith
- Cape Cornwall to Penberth

SIH   Lena and Donald Bray: *St Ives Heritage* (1981; revised edition 1992,
Landfall Publications)

StJP   Edith M. Nicholas: *St Just and Pendeen* (St Just and Pendeen Old
Cornwall Society, 1968)

StJinP John Buller: *A Statistical Account of the Parish of Saint Just in
Penwith in the County of Cornwall, with some Notice of its
Ecclesiastical and Druidical Antiquities*
(1840. Facsimile edition by Dyllansow Truran, 1983)

SWE   Aileen Fox: *South West England* (1964. "Ancient Peoples and
Places" series, Thames & Hudson)

TD   Alison Symons: *Tremedda Days, A View of Zennor, 1900-1944*
(Tabb House, 1992)

TTB   J. A. Buckley: *Tudor Tin Bounds, West Penwith* (Truran, 1987)

WEMR J. H. Collins: *Observations on the West of England Mining Region*
(1912. Reprinted in 1988 by Cornish Mining Classics, Truro)

WFWC Jean Nankervis: *Wicca, A Farm in West Cornwall*
(Revised edition, 1991 - privately published)

WHR   Gerald and Sylvia Priestland: *West of Hayle River* (Wildwood
House, 1980). Republished as *Priestlands' Cornwall*
(Grafton, 1992)

WW   Des Hannigan: *Wildlife Walkabouts: Land's End Peninsula,
Cornwall* (Wayside Books, 1986)

LANDFALL WALKS BOOKS
OTHER VOLUMES IN THE SERIES

> ## *FOR MORE DELIGHTFUL WALKS NOT FAR FROM THE AREA COVERED BY THIS BOOK, SEE ESPECIALLY VOLUMES 4, 6 AND 12.*

No. 1   A VIEW FROM CARN MARTH, Seven Walks amid Cornwall's Industrial Past (1989) 52 pages, £2.50 (Now out of print)

No. 2   A VIEW FROM ST AGNES BEACON, Eight Walks amid Cornwall's Industrial Past (1989) 68 pages, £2.75

No. 3 AROUND THE FAL Circular Walks (1989, revised 1991) 62 pages, £2.95.

No. 4   AROUND THE HELFORD, Circular Walks (1989, reprinted with slight revisions 1990) 64 pages, £2.95

No. 5   AROUND NEWQUAY Circular Walks from Bedruthan to Holywell (1990, revised 1993) 80 pages, £3.30

No. 6   A VIEW FROM CARN BREA, Circular Walks around Redruth, Camborne and Portreath (1990) 80 pages, £2.95

No. 7 AROUND THE RIVER FOWEY, Circular Walks (1990, fully revised and reset 1992) 80 pages, £3.30.

No. 8   AROUND PADSTOW Circular Walks from Porthcothan to Wadebridge and Bodmin   (1991) 68 pages, £3.30

No. 9   A SECOND VIEW FROM CARN MARTH 14 Round Walks near Truro, Falmouth and Redruth (1991) 144 pages including 26 colour photographs, £4.95

No. 10 AROUND ST AUSTELL Circular Walks from Pentewan to Par (1992) 68 pages including 10 colour photographs, £3.30.

No. 11 AROUND MEVAGISSEY Circular Walks from Portscatho to Pentewan   (1992) 84 pages including 8 colour photographs, £3.30

No. 12   A VIEW FROM TRENCROM, Round Walks near Hayle, St Ives and Penzance (1992) 96 pages, £3.30

OTHER LANDFALL BOOKS
THE LANDFALL BOOK OF TRURO (1990) 16 pages, £1.25
THE LANDFALL BOOK OF THE POLDICE VALLEY
(1990)   72 pages including 8 in full colour, £3.99
ST IVES HERITAGE by LENA & DONALD BRAY
(1981, revised 1992) 117 pages including many old photographs, £5.99
NEWQUAY'S PICTORIAL PAST   (1981, revised 1993)
65 photographs from the Woolf/Greenham Collection, £3.00

ALL THE ABOVE BOOKS ARE AVAILABLE IN LOCAL SHOPS
OR CAN BE ORDERED DIRECT FROM THE PUBLISHER
AT THE ADDRESS GIVEN ON PAGE 2.
Please add 60p per book towards postage and packing.
(This is based on 1993 postal costs.)